WRITING
WITH THE
MASTER

WRITING
WITH THE
MASTER

How One of the World's Bestselling Authors
Fixed My Book and Changed My Life

Tony Vanderwarker

SKYHORSE PUBLISHING

Skyhorse Publishing books may be purchased in bulk at special discounts for sales promotion, corporate gifts, fund-raising, or educational purposes. Special editions can also be created to specifications. For details, contact the Special Sales Department, Skyhorse Publishing, 307 West 36th Street, 11th Floor, New York, NY 10018 or info@skyhorsepublishing.com.

Skyhorse® and Skyhorse Publishing® are registered trademarks of Skyhorse Publishing, Inc.,® a Delaware corporation.

Visit our website at www.skyhorsepublishing.com.

10 9 8 7 6 5 4 3 2 1

Library of Congress Cataloging-in-Publication Data is available on file.

ISBN: 978-1-62636-552-0

Printed in the United States

for

ANNIE

CONTENTS

ACKNOWLEDGMENTS

Without John Grisham's generosity of spirit, endless patience, and devotion to the craft of writing (not to mention the countless hours he spent scribbling in the margins of my manuscripts, writing critiques, and imparting his wisdom over countless lunches), this book would not have been possible. Had I paid closer attention and been less impatient, I'm certain my novel, *Sleeping Dogs*, would have initially met a better fate in the marketplace. For when I went back to writing after having hung it up for three years, the additional perspective enabled me not only to use John's guidelines and principles to draft a much better version of *Sleeping Dogs*, but also to write this book.

Few authors hit it out of the park the first time at bat. It's taken me twenty years just to get on base. But in that time, I've made lots of good friends, many of whom have helped me in ways they couldn't imagine. Trish taught me about paydirt, and Claire about persistence, and the many readers I've had over the years have given me both inspiration and guidance. My thanks go to Ralph, Steve, and the members of my men's group, Tom, Dan, Joe, Bob, and Bruce.

My wife Annie, my kids Bryan, Tina, Krissy, Keith, and Vandy, and my brother Pete and his wife Richie have backstopped me and emotionally picked me up and dusted me off when necessary throughout the past twenty years of rolling the writing rock uphill.

I must also mention Sharon Bially, my publicist, who expertly softened the ground for my launch, and David Moody, my Internet guru, who taught me the skills of social networking.

And the folks at Seedhouse, including Bryan, Andrew, Meredith, and Krissy, who came up with the knockout cover designs for all my books.

Holly Rubino, my editor at Skyhorse, made invaluable last-minute contributions to the manuscript as well as helping make the decision to also publish *Sleeping Dogs*.

And last but not least, my agent, Esmond Harmsworth, the man with the marvelous moniker who's been my trusty guide through the roller coaster ride of present-day publishing. He bought into it when no one else got it, put up with my pestering, and saw both books through to acquisition.

Malcolm Gladwell, in an article on late bloomers in *The New Yorker* a few years ago, wrote, "But sometimes genius is anything but rarefied; sometimes it's just the thing that emerges after twenty years of working at your kitchen table."

That's been my story, and I feel damned lucky to have lived it.

INTRODUCTION

Critics love to bash bestselling authors, turning their works into cultural kickballs, labeling their novels "beach reads" and "potboilers," almost as if something that sells a million copies by definition can't have any literary value. Authors like John Grisham and James Patterson, Dan Brown and Stephen King are looked down upon (someone once dubbed King a "horror hack") even as readers flock to bookstores to snap up their newest novels, while the highbrow literary authors, though lionized by critics, often struggle to earn a living from their books.

The cultural elite's disdain for wildly popular novels is perverse and nonsensical. A novel is, after all, a story, and an artfully constructed tale that engages millions ought to be appreciated, just as buildings that are imaginatively designed and beautiful to look at are fawned over. But somehow the museums and towers of architects like Frank Gehry and Santiago Calatrava are lauded to the skies, while the endlessly absorbing and ingenious plots and stories in novels like *The DaVinci Code* or *The Firm* are virtually ignored and dismissed.

If readers are to get anything out of my experience writing with John Grisham other than a healthy dose of my artistic angst and the story of my personal retooling, I hope it will be an appreciation for the craft and expertise required to construct and realize powerful plots. It's not a discipline that's emphasized at the Iowa Writers' Workshop or in college creative-writing courses. Even after as much time as I have spent listening to John's war stories about novel writing, I had little understanding of the diligence, dedication, imagination, and effort he puts into authoring them. Part of it is John's inclination to act as if writing novels is as easy as falling off a log. The ideas just come to him, and he knocks them out one by one. I guess he's going with the flow, in a sense. If people readily dismiss his works as "popular fiction," why should he act as if it's a real craft?

But it is a craft and a demanding and complicated one at that. I learned that lesson the hard way. John's wife, Renée, once challenged me after I'd finished unfairly demeaning and trivializing a huge bestseller. She said, "If you think it's so easy, you try writing one."

CHAPTER 1

This Will Be Fun

I'll never forget the day John Grisham made an offer that launched me on a wild ride full of twists and turns and ups and downs, a two-year odyssey that led me in new and unexpected directions.

We'd chitchatted about writing off and on since we'd become friends, usually about his writing, seldom about mine, since he turns out one or sometimes two bestsellers a year, and I'm still struggling to get my first published.

"How's your novel writing going?" John asks me one day. It's noon, late October 2004. We're sitting in one of our favorite lunch places in downtown Charlottesville eating smart—sole or something—iced tea and water, no booze.

"Okay. Fiddling around with ideas for a new one," I say, putting on a brave face when I'm actually licking wounds from the last barrage of rejection slips and pondering whether

I should take up competitive croquet or plant a vineyard rather than embark on another novel.

Then he says something that knocks me off my feet. "Look, I'd be willing to help you if you'd like. Kind of mentor you through the novel-writing process. Something I've never done before—not that plenty of people haven't asked."

"That would be . . . great," I stammer. *Holy shit! John Grisham wants to help me write a novel!* The thought of working with him had lurked in the back of my mind since we'd become friends, but I never felt it was my prerogative to ask.

"The people in New York I've talked to say you're ninety percent there." "But I have to warn you," John says, and it feels like the other shoe is going to drop. "The last ten percent is the hardest."

"I hear you," I say, but then I'm thinking, *Hell, how hard can it be if John's helping me along?* We've become buddies over the past six years, not just the two of us but also Renée and my wife, Anne. John's nicknamed Anne and me "the VWs," and we've partied and traveled together, attended our kids' school functions, and shared holidays with our families.

On the surface, John and I are unlikely friends. I grew up in a ritzy Connecticut suburb, while John's family had a hardscrabble life cotton farming in Arkansas, which he eloquently captured in *A Painted House.* As you know from looking at his dust jackets, John's Hollywood handsome, has great blue eyes and a full head of hair. I come in second in the looks department and am way behind when it comes to what's up top. But we have common interests in politics and the environment, like to yuck it up and have a couple of beers. We both love good food, especially stinky cheese, and are devoted to our children. And then there's this writing thing. I'm a junker Ford and John's a finely tuned Ferrari, *but what the hell?* I figure. *Let's go for it, could be a blast.*

John doesn't waste any time. "Okay, first we need a story," and this is where Grisham's yarn-spinning motor kicks in. I've seen it many times before. Even sitting around shooting the bull, his tales are masterful, beginning, middle, and end, laced with wry, often sardonic humor, and peppered with engaging personalities. I'm going to see examples of his prolific and versatile imagination over and over again throughout the next two years. Dozens of ideas for plots, techniques to move the story forward in a captivating way, creating quirky traits that make characters come alive—everything starts with a kind of wry smile and a slight cock of his head. Then he lets it rip.

He goes on, "They say you're supposed to write about what you know best. You're an ad guy, so what if we have an out-of-work account exec in D.C., who has a wife and kids and no way to make the mortgage. The job picture is lousy and it's coming up on Christmas and he's at his wit's end, literally desperate. And then out of the blue he gets a call. Someone wants to interview him for a big job selling a product he's never heard of. As you can expect, he doesn't ask a lot of questions, and they hire him, and now he's happier than a pig in you-know-what, so he goes out and charges up a bunch of Christmas presents for the wife and kids. Of course the people who hire him are running a money-laundering scheme. Mafia or something . . ."

I'm not about to tell John Grisham that he's defrosting the plot from his novel *The Firm*, but he sees I'm not jumping up and down, so he takes another bite of sole and tosses the idea away with a quick, "But that's just one of many. You said you had a couple. I'd be happy to hear them."

I can feel myself start to sweat. *Here I am pitching ideas to John Grisham. I'd presented a million ideas before when I was in the ad biz and it was always a breeze, but now I'm on shaky ground trying to sell plot ideas to one of the bestselling authors of all time.*

I quickly sketch out the first.

John takes a sip of tea and shakes his head. "Nope, not compelling enough, too weak, will never work," he says, "Any more?"

I launch into the second, beads of sweat welling up on my forehead.

"Nah," John says before I'm even halfway through, as if sorting through plot ideas is like shopping for ties. "Too complicated."

"Okay, " I say. "Let me try one more on you."

"Sure."

"Our Air Force used to have nuclear weapons in the air at all times, 24/7, so in case of a Russian launch, they'd be able to strike back."

"Yeah, so . . ." John says, giving me space and time.

"So they lost a bunch."

"You're kidding me?" For the first time in the past couple minutes Grisham is engaged. He cocks his head slightly forward as if to listen more intently.

"Dead serious. Ten or twelve, lost them in mid-air collisions, dropped them in the drink by mistake. There's supposed to be one off the coast of Tybee Island in Georgia, another in Alaska. They jettisoned a bomb on some farm in North Carolina—had to quarantine the impact site and pay off the farmer. Of course, the Pentagon claims they're harmless, that the radioactive stuff has disintegrated from being buried in the mud and under thousands of feet of water."

"Whoever heard of a harmless nuke?" John asks, smiling as he swigs his tea. "What if a bad guy got his hands on one of these nukes? Somehow recovered it."

"There you go," I say, making headway for the first time.

John's nodding now as he swipes up some sauce with a crust of bread. "Okay, I like that. Now there's a real idea. Good place to start."

Just as I'm starting to feel very proud of myself, John sets me straight with, "So David says about your characters, 'I don't like his people.'" David Gernert is John's literary agent, used to be his editor at Doubleday until John's agent croaked and John asked Gernert to switch roles. I can't imagine that was a long conversation. Want to make a low six-figure salary toiling away in a publishing house or sit back and take a nice cut of Grisham's royalties? John had graciously offered to connect me with David a couple of years before.

Getting an agent is a major hurdle for an aspiring novelist, and getting picked up, or even considered, by someone as high up in the publishing pantheon as David Gernert is big stuff. I'd submitted my third comic novel to him, and a number of people in his office liked it, so he took a look. He called to tell me he thought it was pretty good ("Funny as hell in a lot of places"), and though it had a couple of problems, he said he was going to take it home with him over the weekend and figure them out.

"I'm pretty good at that," David reassured me. Needless to say, I was scraping myself off the ceiling, my imagination firing up visions of auctions with publishing houses vying for my book, six-figure advances, and movie deals. That Saturday Anne and I had dinner with the Grishams, and when I told them about David's reaction, Renée fueled my exhilaration by saying, "That's huge." I was on cloud nine and ready to crack open the champagne.

Then came David's call early Monday morning. "Tony, I read it again," he said, "and I'm going to pass on it. I'm afraid it's a one-trick pony, to use a phrase from your book. But, if it's any consolation, you should know that this is the first time that my people have been split on a submission." *Close only counts in hand grenades*, I thought as David went on to talk about how divided the agents in his shop were about my novel. "But good luck with it. I'm sure you'll find someone who'll fall in love with it," David finished and said goodbye.

I pitched it to I don't know how many agents over the next year, but no one fell in love, and *Say Something Funny* ended up sleeping soundly in the far reaches of my hard drive.

John continues talking about character development. "So you have to get over David's problem with your people. Your hero, you have to have someone readers want to root for right from the start. You have to ask yourself, 'Are my readers going to like this guy?' Need someone who's interesting, you follow him along until he does something unexpected but within his nature to get your readers engaged, and then what you do is you put people's lives at stake, or everything but their lives, and your central character gets them out of the mess. That's the way it works."

Makes sense. Likeable characters, I've heard that before. I'm giddy, sitting in a restaurant getting the secrets of novel writing from one of the most renowned authors of modern times. Like listening to Shakespeare giving you the ins and outs of how to construct a play. And though I didn't know it then, I'd hear it many times in the future.

"So let's talk about plot. Here's the way popular fiction works. You've got three acts. First is the setup. The novel has to get off to a fast start. Then comes the second act, that's the hard part, the 200 pages in the middle of the novel that have to keep it going without overcomplicating it. And then you've got the ending. That's why you do an outline, so you're sure you're getting off the blocks fast, you've got enough in the middle to make a 360-page book, and then an ending that doesn't run out of gas."

John changes gears. "So I see your story as taking place over a short period of time, one month . . . two or three . . . things happening fast. Maybe you have an ex-CIA guy with a grudge who wants to embarrass the Pentagon over the lost nukes. It's part accident, part cover-up. The Pentagon and CIA are great targets, everyone loves to hate them."

Ex-CIA guy, embarrass the Pentagon, part accident, part cover-up. I'm jotting down notes like mad, praying I don't miss anything.

"So do an outline," John says, tossing down his napkin and getting up from the table. We're splitting lunch like we always do. I toss down a five to sweeten the tip and we head out of the restaurant.

Nice fall day outside, just before Thanksgiving, with temperatures in the mid-sixties. The weather in Charlottesville is one of its most appealing aspects and one of the many reasons Grisham and I moved our families here, at about the same time, in the early '90s, though we didn't become friends until a couple years later when our sons played football together.

He dedicated his novella, *Bleachers*, to the team after they won their second state championship. A tiny private school with fifty boys in a class goes up against giants with five times the students and goes undefeated two years in a row. We had some great times chasing the team around Virginia and cheering them on.

John starts down the hill toward his office. My car's parked in the opposite direction.

"Wait, one thing I forgot," he turns to say. "A synopsis, first you need to do a three-sentence synopsis. Encapsulate the plot, do that before you start the outline." We shake hands, then John smiles and adds, "This will be fun."

"You bet," I say, trying to curb my enthusiasm and thinking, *Damn right! This is the break I've been waiting for. After ten years of rejections and runarounds from agents and publishers, John Grisham's going to help me get a novel off the ground!*

"So how was lunch?" Anne asks when I get home.

"Oh, nothing much." I throw in a pause and then say, "Remember that idea I had about the lost nukes?"

"Yeah, sure . . ." she says tentatively. I've pitched so many ideas to her it's no wonder this one isn't registering.

"John liked it and offered to help me with it."

"Help? How?"

"Help me write it. 'Mentor me' is how he described it."

"You're kidding."

"It came right out of the blue. Asked me how my writing was going. Told him I was working on a couple ideas for a new book, and he offered to help."

"Aren't we lucky to have friends like that?"

"Tell me about it. I feel like I've won the damn lottery."

"Honey, that's terrific! I'm excited for you," Anne says, giving me a big smack on the cheek. She's been a champ over the past ten years, listening to endless one-sided conversations about my characters, plots, and dreams for my novels; encouraging me to enjoy my writing, instead of having an eye on fame or fortune. Reading countless drafts and finished versions; keeping fingers crossed when I submitted manuscripts; and then picking me up and dusting me off when the rejections came in.

"It's okay, Tony. It's part of the process," she'd say as I'd tear open another envelope with the form letters agents regularly send out to writers. "Dear Mr. Vanderwarker,

Unfortunately, your manuscript does not fit into our . . . yadda, yadda, yadda."

John has told me about the shoulder-high stacks of unread novels he's seen sitting around Gernert's office. He knows too well the struggle most aspiring writers face. Lucky to find an agent and get his first book, *A Time to Kill,* published, John peddled copies out of the trunk of his car to bookstores and anyone who would buy them. And he readily admits good fortune played a part in getting Doubleday to pick up his second, *The Firm.* Turns out a reader at a New York publishing house was being paid under the table by a Hollywood studio to be on the lookout for novels that could be turned into films. The reader sent it out to the Coast, and word started getting around. A producer made an option offer. I remember a number like six hundred grand. The buzz about the option got David Gernert's attention at Doubleday. He read the manuscript and quickly made an offer. And when it was published that winter, as luck would have it, there were not many competing thrillers on the market, so it zoomed to the top of the bestseller list. The rest is history. John folded his law practice and started writing full time.

"How's this going to work?" she asks.

"Not sure. I guess we'll play it by ear. He wants me to write a three-sentence synopsis first, then start on an outline." *A three-sentence synopsis, how hard can that be? Should be a piece of cake,* I think to myself.

CHAPTER 2

Some Piece of Cake

The synopsis gives me a false sense of security. John okays it, gives me a few pointers, and tells me to start the outline. I dive in, writing five hours a day, six days a week. *How hard can this be? It's an outline, not the Magna Carta.*

John told me once that on a good day he gets five pages of a novel written. Under a deadline, he wrote one book from start to finish in three months. Usually takes him five. I project out. Here we are in late October. Give me a couple weeks to get the outline done, should have the manuscript completed say, mid-March or the first of April. After years of rejection, I'm already starting to smell the barn. I crank it out in a week.

I fell in love with the idea of writing novels sometime in high school. I went to prep school outside of Boston during the tail end of the Eisenhower years and caught the writing bug from J. D. Salinger and *The Catcher in the Rye*. I'd come from an upper-middle class Fairfield County, Connecticut family. My father was an insurance executive, and my parents' social set was mostly businessmen who worked in New York and their upwardly mobile wives. As a precocious teenager in the dull and dreary late '50s, I thought my parents and their friends had walked right out of a John Cheever story—they were superficial and one dimensional, only interested in golf, cocktail parties, careers, and keeping up with the Joneses.

Being a novelist had a romantic allure. The idea of being Salinger sitting in a cabin in upstate New York turning out bestsellers was a dramatic contrast to the pedestrian, mercantile pursuits of my parents.

Other than daydream about it, I did little writing aside from college term papers and essays until I joined the Peace Corps. Assigned to a hole-in-the-wall town in the middle of the sub-Saharan savanna, I had lots of time on my hands, so I wrote reams of ersatz Rimbaud poetry and took a crack at a couple of novels. Going through the stuff ten years later, I laughed at my youthful pretension and chucked everything in the trash.

After the Peace Corps, I went into the film business, starting as a messenger carrying cans of film around Manhattan, becoming an editor, then a director making documentaries and industrial films and, finally, a full-length dramatic film.

Convinced I was shooting the next *Easy Rider*, I spent two years working on it, raising money, filming and editing it, and trying to sell it to distributors. For a low-budget picture, it had lavish production values—35mm color, special effects, a music track—it was only missing a good script. I remember the projectionist coming out of the booth after our first screening. Though the entire audience of film moguls had walked out before the end of the first reel, he handed me the cans of film and cheerily said, "Don't worry about it. I screened Stanley Kubrick's first film here, and the same thing happened. And look at his career."

The movie never made it to the big screen, and, broke and disillusioned, I took a job in advertising, putting my motion picture experience to work producing commercials. I did TV spots for McDonalds, Bud Light, Busch beer, while I worked myself up through the creative ranks, eventually ending up with my own agency where we did the "Be Like Mike" campaign for Gatorade.

As successful as I had become, I still had the nagging desire to write novels. So when my partners offered to buy me out, I jumped at the chance. I remember thinking, *Sayonara, advertising, now it's novel-writing time!* Ever since reading *The Firm* five years before, I had watched Grisham's meteoric rise to the top of the bestseller charts and figured, *Hell, if a small-town lawyer can do it, why can't Tony?*

I uprooted the family from our fancy digs in Chicago and moved to a small farm outside of Charlottesville, with a detached summer kitchen that looked like the ideal perch for writing the Great American Novel. My wife was enthusiastic about relocating to Virginia as her folks lived nearby, and she was tired of city living and felt our kids were growing up too quickly there. The children kicked and screamed, convinced we had wrecked their lives.

About the same time, Grisham found his writing cabin on a farm a few miles south of ours and moved his family up from Mississippi. Some ten years later, we're now collaborating on a novel.

I keep pinching myself as I work on the outline, walking on air knowing that John Grisham is shepherding me along in the book-writing process. Even after we became friends, though I might have dreamed of working together, I'd never imagined that it would come to pass. The closest we'd come was when Gernert was toying with my *Say Something Funny* novel, and Renée had casually suggested that John and I might team up on a screenplay. When David rejected my book, the movie idea went up in smoke.

Here and there, I got glimpses of what it's like to be a famous novelist when we were rushed out of a limo through crowds eager to get John's autograph, or when I was standing with John in a supermarket checkout line at the beach when a lady approached him and tentatively asked, "Excuse me, are you John Grisham?"

John chortled and said, "No, no, no, that happens all the time."

She seemed relieved. "I didn't think so. I couldn't imagine John Grisham shopping in a Food Lion."

As I waded into the outline, any giddy feeling was soon elbowed out of the way by a discomforting realization: *I'm on soft ground with this outline, not really sure of what I'm doing.* My other books I made up as I went along, allowing the characters to drive the action while I sat back and wondered to myself, *okay, what happens next?* While I had a vague plot in mind and sometimes an ending, I'd always thought of writing as a free-form experience, letting the plot drive itself with just a few course corrections now and then. And a twelve-week fiction-writing course in Manhattan taught by Gordon Lish, as well as two summer sessions at Sewanee and one at Bennington, confirmed that was the way novels are written. Plots were seldom mentioned, thought of as prosaic and pedestrian compared to the lofty task of creating characters and crafting prose. Plotted fiction was fast food—crammed with clichéd dialogue and stock characters out of some hack's impaired imagination.

Over beers at the writing camps, I used to get into heated arguments about John's fiction. "His characters are cardboard, dialogue next to doggerel," I remember one of my fellow campers bleating.

"Maybe," I countered, "but my bet is his plots will hold up for a hundred years. He'll be right up there with Dickens and Stevenson. Just because an author imposes an order on life doesn't invalidate his or her work," I continued. "As the English novelist Ivy Compton-Burnett once said, 'As regards plot I find real life no help at all. Real life seems to have no plot. And as I think a plot desirable and almost necessary, I have this extra grudge against life.' Plots are stories, and stories are why people read. That's why Grisham sells millions of books."

The debate would end with some highly contemptuous sneer from a camper like, "Yeah, with crappy prose and a plot about a Mafia law firm, c'mon."

In the end, for the aspiring literary novelists, it all came down to money. John makes too much for them to take him seriously.

But John is dead serious about plots and outlines. I think back to one day when we were shooting the breeze about writing, and John asked me, "You do outlines for your novels, don't you?" in much the same tone as if he'd asked, "You always buckle your seat belt, right?" Not wanting to appear undisciplined, I glibly answered, "Oh, sure." And he came back with, "I couldn't imagine writing a book without first doing an outline." John's hardly a somber guy, but he doesn't kid around about outlines.

Even looks down his nose at undisciplined writers, once mentioning with disdain a certain famous novelist who ships stacks of pages to his editor, who then in turn faces the daunting task of cutting and pasting to assemble a book from the disorganized mess. But that's John, always precise in his thinking and perfectly put together in his appearance, even if he's out in the heat striping a baseball diamond. His everyday uniform of pressed jeans and jaunty Italian sport coats has shamed me into abandoning my slovenly country look, much to the delight of my wife. The only thing I've got him on is the quality of our eyeglasses. John insists on wearing cheapie drugstore readers, while I sport a variety of stylish Philippe Starck frames.

I sit in my studio staring at the scenery. But today it's not giving me much inspiration. Struggling to craft this damn outline, I'm feeling like Wile E. Coyote running off a cliff with my feet pedaling like mad and nothing but air beneath.

It's the hardest, most demanding writing I've ever done. Not really writing, more like constructing a building, pouring one floor, putting up the walls, and moving up to the next. I find myself groping in the dark for the next turn of the plot. Paragraph after paragraph of the outline describing what will happen in the novel—before I've even written it.

I'm relieved when I finally sketch out the last episode.

I've got the hero, Jock Caldwell, a sympathetic, Kennedyesque character with a successful State Department career specializing in disarmament until he steps on one too many toes with his preoccupation with lost nukes and gets bounced out. Starts a campaign to recover one of the bombs, actually finds it, and comes up with a plot to blackmail the five members of the nuclear club. He crafts exact replicas and ships them to the five countries in the club. Posing as a terrorist, he sends an email to the president of the United States and the leaders of the other countries with a photo of the one he recovered. He demands they stop development of nuclear weapons, put all existing devices under UN control, and fund a joint effort to recover all missing nukes. Since they can't be sure a live one isn't lurking within their borders, the five give in. The details of the blackmail plot are covered up to protect everyone concerned, a crisis is averted, and Caldwell becomes a hero.

Certain I've nailed it, I drop it off at John's office, hardly able to wait for his reaction.

A couple of days later, John calls, and I rush into town to pick up his notes. I can't wait to read them, ripping open the envelope as soon as I'm in the car.

I remember having the same feeling at a championship lacrosse game in high school when I thought I had rocketed the ball into the net after quickly dodging a defender with a world-class move. Expecting to hear jubilation from the crowd, I heard only the panting of my teammates as they ran down the field chasing the opponent who'd scooped up the ball that had fallen out of my stick.

Here's what John's letter said:

JOHN GRISHAM   November 6, 2004

        re: Sleeping Dogs

Tony:

I'm not an editor, and I've never gone through this process before.
The only way it might work is that we - especially me - decide not
to pull punches.

My first reaction to the outline to say "Slow down." You have a
hyperactive imagination. It can be an asset, but it can also take
your eye off the ball.

There's too much going on. Most plots fail because they get too
complicated. It's not easy to keep one simple, but it's crucial.
A strong central plot that stays on track can afford the luxury of
spinning off subplots, but not too many.

You need to go back to the very basics - pitch the story in one
small paragraph,   something like -

     "On March 12, 1958, a hydrogen bomb was jettisoned in
     the Atlantic near Tybee Island, Georgia. It was the 10th
     known nuclear warhead lost by the Pentagon. Jock Caldwell,
     a disgraced CIA analyst, finds it, recovers it, and for
     20 days holds the world hostage . . . . .

     or something like that

The next step is to set this outline aside, and do another one.
Something completely different. This story has so much potential,
it can be told in several different plots. Let's look at another
one. There's plenty of time.

I'm feeling part embarrassment, part dread, some anger, and a dose of insecurity mixed in—a whole stew of nasty emotions. Rejection doesn't bring out one's best qualities.

"The next step is to set this outline aside." John had written. "Let's look at another one." *I blew it. He didn't like anything.* Throw this one out and start over, John's saying. *Two weeks down the drain . . . hardly got anything right.*

The rest of his comments are equally painful.

```
Like a lot of stories, the setup is great.  The difficult part is
maintaining the tension for 200 pages, then blowing away the reader
with an ending that no one can predict.

Now that I've said all that, allow me to comment on the outline:

Act One:
---------------------------
    1.   It's very tricky to cover 40 years in a few chapters.
    2.   Think about squeezing the time frame dramatically, and
         keeping the entire story in, say, 1972, during the
         Cold War.  It doesn't have to be contemporary.
    3.   There's too much of Jock.  Ruined career, broken
         marriage, potential suicide.  This might work if it
         takes place over the course of the story, but it's too
         much too early.
    4    I think you told me that there was really a bomb near
         Savannah.  If this is so, then I'd stay away from there
         and find another spot - say the outer banks or the
         eastern shore of Va.
    5.   With a strong factual background (10 lost bombs) you
         need to work hard to stay away from real names and
         places.
    6.   Same for Jock Caldwell.  If he's even close to a real
         person, then you're dead.
    7.   For that reason, try another hero in the next outline
         Someone completely different.

             A thought - What about the pilot who ditches the
             bomb?  After the midair collision, he's told to
             ditch the bomb, which he does, then he manages
             to parachute out, the plane crashes in the ocean
             and all are presumed dead.  The Pentagon does a
             massive coverup on all fronts.  The young pilot
             rescues himself in the mountains somewhere, say
             North Carolina, finds an empty cabin, slowly
             gets himself back together.  When he's able to
             find out what happened, he realizes he's already
             been memorialized, dead, covered up, buried under
             a flood of Pentagon lies.

             But they're looking for him.  And he's looking for
             the bomb, which obviously didn't detonate.

             Maybe he finds the Jock Caldwell character.
```

```
Act Two:
---------------------------

1.   To make five bombs, transport them to five countries,
successfully bury them, etc., would take too much ink.  This is
where the story starts to drift, and it never gets back on track.


Act Three
---------------------------
1.   I'm not much on Hollywood endings, where the hero gets
rewarded, etc.  But they do work.  Let's talk about it.

2.   Everything comes together too neatly for Jock.  After being
such a scoundrel and terrifying the world,  he wouldn't be allowed
to become such a hero.

3.   I can't suggest an ending - that's not my job here.  But it's

one reason I'd like to see a new outline.




I don't know if I told you, but I pitched the premise to Renee one
night.  She's heard a hundred of my little pitches over the years,
and she's very good at a quick thumbs up or down.  She's almost
always right.

She really likes this story.  I believe in it too.  One problem
with it, though, is that it can go in so many directions.  Let's
try and find a solid, basic plot.

Keep working and good luck.
```

"What's the matter?" my wife asks when I walk in the door. I hand her the three pages without a word.

She skims it quickly and says, "So what's the problem?"

"What's the problem? He hated it, he's telling me to start over."

"So? He likes the story. That's what counts. He even pitched it to Renée, and she liked it. I don't see what you're so upset about."

"He cut the thing to ribbons."

"I told you the five bombs thing was too much."

"Wait a minute, whose side are you on?"

"Don't go there, okay?" she cautions. My wife is no weak sister. And I know I'm crossing the line.

"Okay," I say, retreating quickly.

"Do what John says and start a new one. What's so hard about that?"

"I just thought I'd nailed it."

"Well, you didn't, so get over it. Now get dressed for dinner, Mr. Big-time Novelist. We're going over to Mother's, remember?" She also cautions me, "The last thing she wants to hear about is this outline business. So can it, okay?"

Having a couple glasses of wine and engaging in a little chitchat will help me climb over my debacle, I decide. My mother-in-law lives in an old-folks home a couple of miles away. She has her own house, a two-bedroom job that's bright and airy. We joke that these communities are like Dante's stages of hell. There are homes for those still mobile, the apartments people move to when they get creaky, and finally the assisted-living facility for those who are bedridden or lose their marbles.

Ellie loves to yuck it up about the place. She talks about "winterkill," the rapid decline in the population caused by snow and ice, how whenever a new man moves in women flock around him like vultures, and getting accustomed to people dying. "Happens so often around here, it's no big deal anymore." When she hears something ridiculous or shocking, Ellie's favorite expression, delivered in a mock evangelist's tone of voice, is, "Oh Lord, help me to pray." And she's full of eighty-eight years' worth of stories, like when the circus came to town, and since her father was mayor they'd pause in front of her house. Ellie's a great sport, with a twinkle in her eyes, and a trenchant sense of humor matched with an infectious laugh. I adore the lady, particularly since my own mother's insecurity walled her emotions in and kept her feelings in check. Ellie, on the other hand, generously ladles out emotion, and I always come away with a feeling of well-being.

She's also a good cook and has a well-stocked bar, so it's always a delight to visit.

"C'mon in, dears. So good to see you," Ellie says as she opens the door for us. "Come fix yourselves a drink, and then sit down and tell me everything you've been doing. I can't wait to hear." You have to look beyond the white hair, wrinkles, wattles, stooped shoulders, and shuffling gait to see her beauty, but when Ellie smiles it all comes back.

She laps up our latest news, the childrens' adventures, the goings-on around the farm, and local gossip. As I'm getting up to refresh my glass, Ellie says, "So how's your writing with Mr. Grisham going?"

I can't resist shooting a smirk at my wife as I put on a brave face and answer, "Not bad, but he's a tough taskmaster."

"I could have told you that going in. You've really got your work cut out for you. But if anyone can do it, Tony, you can!"

That's Ellie for you. A healthy dose of reality capped off with a nice pat on the back.

The next day, having read John's notes fifty times, me and my hyperactive imagination are back at the keyboard. Having been in the advertising business for almost twenty years, I've had my feet kicked out from under me more times than I can remember. But those were just ads, silly compared to a novel outline with my ego firmly attached, and now it's bruised and battered. I so much wanted to kick it through the uprights for John, show him he's not wasting his time with me, and what do I do? I whiff it entirely.

I'm sitting in my studio staring out the window across the fields at the wooded mountains beyond when suddenly it hits me. Despite all the criticism, John's pointed me in a productive new direction. "A thought—what about the pilot who ditches the bomb?" he asked in his notes.

Of course, I think. *I don't have to have my central character locate the bomb. Since the pilot knows where it is, all I need is my hero to find the pilot.* So much quicker and easier, now I can compress forty years into this old coot who's been hiding in the mountains. My guy tracks him down, and they go searching for the nuke with the Pentagon in hot pursuit. That's the quick timeframe he was talking about.

Now I'm finally getting what he was saying—all that crap about making the five replicas, as John put it, "takes too much ink, this is where the story starts to drift and it never gets back on track."

It dawns on me why an outline is so critical. It provides signposts through the course of the plot that keep the writer on track. If I'd written the novel with the five bombs, I would have lost the reader somewhere along the way and turned out a botched book. John's saving me from myself, giving me a new direction, and even a pat on the back at the end by mentioning Renée liked it. All I have to do is go slow, keep my imagination in check, and find the solid, basic plot John's talking about.

CHAPTER 3

Easier Said Than Done

My studio is high on an oak-studded hill overlooking our farm and the mountains beyond. They're hardly mountains, as the tallest is just a touch over 1200 feet, but since Jefferson's day they've been called the Southwest Mountains, so that's how we refer to them. Mr. Jefferson, which is what we call him around here, built Monticello on one of the peaks, naming it after the Italian for "little mountain."

The building in which I write is a variation on a church steeple. Tall but tiny, twenty-five feet high but only nine feet square with enough space for a writing desk and a couple bookcases packed with reading material for this novel. I write from 8:30 a.m. to noon or so and then spend the rest of the day researching atomic weapons, American nuclear policy during the Cold War, the CIA, our other intelligence agencies, and anything else I can dig up.

Carefully crafting the next outline, I try to be patient though it's killing me. Deliberating each new plot turn and carefully evaluating every scene to makes sure it works. John's caution to *slow down* is scrawled on a sticky at the top of my screen.

I kick it off with a newly elected president of the United States calling the joint chiefs on the carpet to explain why they haven't located the eleven lost thermonuclear weapons. The chiefs stonewall the president, insisting they are unarmed and harmless. Yet while driving back to the Pentagon after the meeting, they talk about the existence of a covert operation code-named "Sleeping Dogs," set up during the '50s to keep a lid on the subject of the lost nukes.

Only my four springer spaniels lounging around on the floor of my studio hear my triumphant *whoop!* as I realize I've come up with the title for my novel. *Sleeping Dogs! Let sleeping dogs lie. It's perfect.*

The outline goes on to have my hero, renamed Howie Chalmers, find the old man whom he suspects might be the pilot of the plane that dropped a device somewhere on the Eastern Seaboard. As he works to connect the pilot to the lost bomb, the Pentagon gets the scent of his quest and starts shadowing him. I devote most of the second act to Howie wheedling the location out of the old guy. He finally reveals the nuke was dropped over the Chesapeake Bay between Baltimore and D.C., threatening the lives of millions. The pieces are falling into place. I'm excited about the progress I'm making. After a month, it's finally taking shape.

One day in late December, I give it a last read and hit PRINT, eager to get it into John's hands before Christmas, as I'm concerned that he's going to be too busy with last-minute holiday stuff to spend time editing my outline.

I give him a ring. "No problem," he says. He jokes that it will give him a good excuse to get away from decorating their tree, and we set up a lunch. John loves to poke fun at all the crazy holiday hoopla. I suspect it gave him the idea for his first short novel, *Skipping Christmas*.

Since it's two days before the holiday, John goes easy on me. He's jovial and relaxed, hands out a couple compliments, and tells me I have a good working title. We have a couple glasses of wine and a pleasant lunch kicking around the outline.

But as I replay his comments from my notes after our lunch, I slowly begin to realize I'm at square one, back to the drawing board for Tony. "Something happens that kicks Chalmers into high gear at the beginning," I read from my notes. "It's the connection with the pilot and his secret that gets the story started." That means canning the opening with the president and the joint chiefs. And ditching the middle with Chalmers trying to connect the aviator with the bomb. It means a new outline with Chalmers finding him right off the bat and uncovering his startling secret. The two hundred pages in the middle are the two of them searching for the bomb with the Pentagon chasing them.

It's no mystery what John's doing. He's chucking out story elements that don't directly relate to the essence of the plot—the bomb and the pilot who knows its location.

Reminds me of a famous pro football player, a defensive end with the wonderful name of Too Tall Jones who, when asked how he always managed to find the ball carrier when a million offensive players were swarming toward him, answered, "I tackle them all and toss them away one by one until I find the guy with the ball."

John works the same way. It's the first Grisham Law of novel writing. Find the locus of your plot. The answer to the question, what is this book really about? The most salient element, the pivot upon which the entire plot revolves. Toss everything else out until you get to the core. *Sleeping Dogs* is not about lost nukes, a bunch of Pentagon generals, or a former Pentagon staffer who's WMD obsessed. It's about a pilot who has a terrible secret. And locating the focal point is like peeling back the leaves of an artichoke, stripping off one and then another until the heart of the plot is revealed. Unless you mine that central plot nugget and bore down on it, your novel will wander all over the place, your reader will never quite figure out what your novel is about, and will eventually set it aside. That is, if you can even get it past an agent and an editor. I recently came across a poll of editors, and the consensus was that weak plots are the most crippling aspect of submitted work. While plots can be weak for lots of reasons, I'd bet a key cause is the writer's failure to pin down the nub.

Thinking back on our last discussion, I'm starting to wonder whether John's figured out the entire plot months ago, and he's leading me along, picking me up when I stumble, brushing me off, and steering me off in the right direction. Or may be he's putting it together as I am. *Is this the process you have to go through to get a story that works?* In any case, I'm already two months into the process, and I'm still peeling artichokes.

"I'd appreciate it if you'd join us for Christmas," my wife says to me later that day. She's loaded for bear. Anne's a reasonable person, but like many of us she tends to get a touch amped up over the holidays, and that's when my minor faults get instantly magnified.

"Of course. Did you think I was going somewhere?"

"That damn novel! You're off in another world. You're leaving everything to me and I'm sick of it, okay?"

"You bet. What can I do?"

"Another thing, no one in the family wants to hear the play-by-play of your latest outline, so do us a favor—for just five days, no *Sleeping Dogs.*"

"I won't say a thing."

"You better not."

And I don't. For five days my lips stay zipped though my brain can't leave it alone. I trim the tree, set a fire, drape lights over the porch rail, complete all the chores on my list. But I also jot down notes like mad. Scribble on stickies and secrete them under a book in the den, hide scraps of paper inside a novel. Don't let a day go by without moving the plot along.

Finally focusing on the nub of my plot, I put the pilot in a VA hospital and have Chalmers discover him there. The old guy's son contacts Chalmers through his lost-nukes website. For some reason, the government has stopped paying his father's hush money. He thinks Chalmers, with his interest in unrecovered bombs, might be able to help. The Defense Department finds out Chalmers has made contact with the pilot. The story starts to pick up pace. Chalmers spirits him out of the VA hospital, and they start the search with the Pentagon hot on their heels.

"Dad, can you pass the yams?" my daughter asks.

"What?" I say, jarred out of my reverie back to the Christmas dinner table. As I reach for the casserole, I check to see if my wife has noticed and is already giving me the evil eye. "Sure, honey, here you go." Fortunately, she hasn't.

I get through Christmas without any missteps and even blow off a question about the novel from one of my sons with a breezy, "Coming along fine, thanks for asking."

A couple weeks later, I'm sitting with John in Oxo, our restaurant of choice for outline lunches. Again, he begins with compliments. He likes my hero, likes the locales of Charlottesville, where Chalmers lives, and the VA hospital in Pittsburgh. He buys Risstup, the old pilot. But he suggests that I change Chalmers's name. "Too complicated," he explains. "You don't want any question of pronunciation or apostrophizing, so pick a simpler one. What I do is pick up the phone book, go through it until I find a name that's familiar but distinctive." Then he stops me in my tracks. "You know, I'm thinking about the plot and a light bulb suddenly goes on. Who in the world would most like to get their hands on a nuke?" It's not hard to figure out where John's eureka moment is taking him.

"Al-Qaeda," I offer.

"They used our own planes as bombs. Cheap, easy to pull off, and absolutely brilliant."

Talk about brilliant, I'm thinking. Instead of complicating the plot with story elements pulled in willy-nilly from left field, he's dimensionalizing it with a germane component. Rather than just Chalmers and the Pentagon, now we add to the mix the group that would most like to locate a bomb within the borders of the United States, giving me a fresh new plot palette to play with.

John starts lobbing concepts at me as he leans across his plate, his brow furrowed, his lips barely able to keep up with the torrent of ideas. It's like I'm standing in front of a batting machine, and balls are flying at me high, low, and inside.

"Here all they have to do is come and get the nuke, or follow Chalmers to it. . . . Al-Qaeda are the worst bad guys you can imagine. Here you have a fifty-year-old problem and a Pentagon cover-up, a stale problem to which no one's paying attention. . . . Al-Qaeda is really watching Chalmers, who's only trying to get to the bottom of the story. . . . See, Risstup is at the VA hospital in Pittsburgh with a secret wing where they put the old spies, Annex Three or something like that. . . . Chalmers gets contacted by a young doctor who has talked to Risstup enough to get the idea he knows where a lost nuke is. He finds Chalmers's website. Doc has to tip off the Pentagon with his call to Howie. When the doc disappears, nurse gets concerned, calls Chalmers, and says the final pill is to be administered. Risstup can't be a complete robot because the doc contacts Howie, so the doc has to have found out something from him. When Risstup doesn't die but disappears instead, the Pentagon wakes up. Once Howie kidnaps Risstup, he and the nurse are on the run."

John's on a roll, spinning out ideas faster than I can jot them down.

"Chalmers is a computer genius. He's got B-52 footage, video game stuff. He figures out where the final flight went, figures it out with Risstup giving him clues. Maybe the old guy's memory is coming back." John finishes his salmon and takes a sip of tea while the waiter scurries back with more scrap paper.

I'm getting this image of John stringing pearls, threading them one by one and sliding them down so they click together and complete a string. It's the second Grisham Law of fiction writing. Develop a straight line of story elements, each logically growing out of the former, nothing tangential that will cause the plot to veer off track and the reader to lose interest and put your novel down.

John resumes his pearl stringing. "You have a suicide diver who can detonate the bomb, do a flashback to al-Qaeda training the suicide diver. And look, Howie can save the world without a big Hollywood ending. He can walk away and go back to Virginia. You've read what the CIA says about their operations: 'You never hear about our big successes.' You have to create this imminent fear, get to al-Qaeda in the third chapter. First chapter is the B-52 accident where the bomb is lost, second is Howie lecturing to a bunch of students at UVa about unrecovered nukes. By pages thirty to forty, the reader knows the bomb is in this country and al-Qaeda is after it, and he's hooked." John sits up. "So that's it in a nutshell. Up to you to take it from there."

"Wow, lot of great stuff here," I say, shuffling my notes together.

"Thanks, I do it for a living, you know," he smiles. *And a pretty good living at that,* I'm thinking. *Couple hundred million books sold at two or three bucks a crack, soon that adds up to some real money. And that's not counting movie sales, audio books—every dollar coming from John's fingers flying over the keyboard.*

When the check's paid, John chucks his napkin on the table and pushes his chair back. "Okay, so three acts, no dialogue. I want to see how you end it."

"Whew," is all I can muster, then, "Thanks," as I grab my notes and we head out of the restaurant.

"Hey, no problem. Like I said, it's a good story," he says, quickly segueing into, "So how's Vandy's upcoming season look?" That's our youngest son who's at college now, recruited to play lacrosse. The two big spring sports in central Virginia are lacrosse and baseball. John's son is a pretty good baseball player, so we go our own ways in the spring.

John is Charlottesville's "Mr. Baseball," having given the community a world-class Little League facility with a bunch of fields, locker rooms, even a refreshment stand, plus an impressive new stadium and softball diamond at our kids' private school as well as dramatically improving the ball field at UVa and helping to recruit a new coach who has taken the program from lame to nationally ranked.

"Looking good. First game's this weekend," I answer.

"You guys going up?" John catches himself, adding, "Now that's a stupid question." My wife and I are the team parents who have organized tailgate picnics for four years.

We take different paths at the next intersection and wave goodbye.

My head is reeling with all the new pearls John has strung for me. Al-Qaeda, suicide diver, the final pill, kidnapping Risstup to save him, escaping with the nurse, Howie being a computer genius, lecturing about the lost bombs at UVa— all plot elements that flow from and relate to one another, are stunningly imaginative and absolutely dead on.

What really amazes me is when John comes up with story-enhancing ideas like having Howie lecture the students about the unrecovered nukes, giving me the opportunity to turn what would have been twenty pages of mind-numbing exposition into absorbing narrative. That's huge.

And to chart out the plot so he knows by pages thirty or forty that the reader has to realize the bomb is in the United States. How does he know that? I guess when you've writ-ten twenty books, it becomes second nature, the instinctive intuition about how to hook a reader. In a flash, I suddenly remember being struck by a similar situation in one of John's earlier books. I rush home, pull out his first legal thriller, *The Firm,* and skim the first forty pages.

Dazzled by oodles of money, a new BMW, and a low-interest mortgage loan, it doesn't occur to the young law grad that there's anything fishy about the mid-sized Memphis firm that's recruiting him. But Grisham begins to drop hints in the second chapter that things are not on the up-and-up at the law firm. And by the end of the third, when Grisham lets the reader in on a conversation between the head of security and a senior partner (first about snooping on the lawyer and his wife in their hotel room, then about killing cops), the reader gets the eerie feeling that the protagonists are heading into a perfect storm.

The reader's hooked and guess what? That's all by page thirty-eight. I've tripped over the third Grisham Law of writing bestsellers: Snare them in the first forty pages and your novel's off to the races.

Gatoring up to my studio with the dogs in the back, I sort through my notes and a disquieting question pops into my head: *I just took four pages of dictation determining the plot of my novel. Who's writing this book anyhow?* It's a question better left unanswered. *You signed up for this gig. Do what John says—three acts, no dialogue. You've got the three laws, so get going.*

CHAPTER 4

Outline Five

It's early February, and I've been writing outlines for three months.

Sitting down at my computer with my notes in front of me, I realize what I'm facing is not a revision; it's start-over time again. The myth of Sisyphus seems an apt metaphor for writing outlines with Grisham. I feel as if I'm pushing the rock uphill with great effort only to have it come tumbling back down again.

Despite what John said about starting with the B-52 accident, I have a better idea. I insert a prologue introducing Osama bin Laden, not by name, but as an unmistakable figure in a headscarf and robes standing alone before a wind-swept cave with an AK-47 slung over his shoulder. Since it's an introduction to the novel, it doesn't have to deal with the nub of the plot, only foreshadow what's going to happen.

I think I've hit a long one, clear over the fence. I'm sure John's going to love it.

I close the scene with, "As he listened to the insistent wind whistling around the mouth of the cave, he remembered the quote from Socrates about swans: 'When they perceive approaching death they sing more merrily than before because of the joy they have in going to the God they serve.' He would have one more chance before he sang merrily, and the beauty of his final act would be horrible."

Feeling like I've set a creepy and ominous tone, I cut to Howie walking down the Lawn at UVa. I've renamed him Howie Collyer—no "s," distinctive and easy to pronounce. And, of course, I make him likeable and reader-friendly.

Delivering a dramatic PowerPoint presentation to a class that sits the students up straight, Howie lays out the case that multiple thermonuclear weapons are scattered around the United States.

Next I introduce the sleeper cell of al-Qaeda terrorists who know from Howie's website that he's obsessed with finding the lost nukes, so they're monitoring it hoping he will lead them to a live one.

Suddenly, a call from a doc at a VA hospital outside of Pittsburgh interrupts Howie's Thanksgiving dinner. One of the patients, named Risstup, has information about a missing bomb that's putting his life in danger.

Rushing to Pittsburgh, Howie gets a call from a nurse saying the doc who alerted him has disappeared, and she has been given a directive to administer a shot that will surely kill Risstup. Substituting a homeless man for Risstup, Howie and the nurse kidnap the old guy and hide out in a seedy nursing home while the scene shifts to al-Qaeda scuba divers training in the Arabian Sea.

The Pentagon kicks into high gear with the news that Collyer has nabbed Risstup, and there are also indications al-Qaeda is tracking him. I add to the suspense with people at a YMCA pool puzzling over why three Arab-looking men are diving with European scuba gear.

At the nursing home, Collyer and the nurse work with computer simulations to help Risstup piece together the bomb's location.

The Secretary of Homeland Security, an old friend of Collyer's who knows of Howie's obsession with lost nukes, begins to suspect he's involved. Confronting the Pentagon, he learns they are chasing Collyer and the terrorists.

Finally, Howie's able to glean from Risstup that the bomb was dropped in the Chesapeake Bay, just miles from D.C. Howie goes after it with al-Qaeda and the Pentagon close on his heels.

I wrap everything up with a knockout ending. A Black Hawk blows up the terrorists as they race toward the bomb location, Howie's a hero, and the Pentagon takes the heat for the cover-up.

I print out the outline and proudly present it to my wife.

"Can I read it later?" she asks.

"Sure," I say, but seeing the disappointment on my face, she picks it up and skims it quickly.

"You've come a long way. You must be pleased."

"Thanks, I just hope John likes it."

"I'm sure he will."

While I wait for John to get back to me, I'm on pins and needles and not much fun to live with. I bug Anne incessantly with questions about the outline. Do you think I handled this right? What about the bomb—do you understand enough about it to appreciate the threat it poses? Does the ending work for you?

After a week's worth of questions, Anne turns to me and says quietly but with no question of her intent, "You know, Tony, you need to get a life." She's been a rock to me for almost thirty years and always supportive but quick to bring me up short when I offload my issues onto her. We've raised four children, ridden the roller coaster of major moves and career shifts, suffered the trauma of losing parents and through it all managed to remain soul mates and close friends, partially because we can call each other when we go off base. We're fortunate to have a sturdy relationship, and much of the credit goes to Anne's nature. She's caring and kind but tough as nails at the same time.

Let me tell you a story to show you what a trooper my wife is. Flash back thirty years ago when we were living in Evanston just outside of Chicago. I was making commercials for McDonalds, and Anne was pregnant with our fourth. Running some errands with our daughter and a couple of our neighbor's kids, she was T-boned at an intersection by a crazoid running a red light. Fortunately everyone was wearing seatbelts, so despite the fact that our car was totaled, there were no injuries save for a small gash on one kid's chin.

Everyone thanked their lucky stars and motored on in a rental car while we filed the insurance claim. That weekend, we were sitting in the living room picking over the paper when my wife looked up at me and said, "You better take me to the hospital, something's wrong."

After making a quick call to her Ob/Gyn, I scooped Anne out of the chair, carried her to the car, and sped to the hospital twenty blocks away.

I vividly remember sitting in a small waiting room blankly watching a rerun of *The Love Boat* when her doc walked in. His face was not full of good news. "I think the baby is going to be all right, I'm not sure about your wife." He went on to explain that they'd started doing a C-section thinking the problem was with the fetus but quickly found a ton of blood in her abdomen. So they halted the Caesarean and called in a surgical team.

"I'll let you know as soon as I find out something," he said, hurriedly closing the door. I was understandably struggling with the turnaround in events while the stupid sitcom blared in the background. *What could have happened to her?* His words, "I'm not sure about your wife," kept ringing in my ears.

I don't remember how long it was, but the doctor returned, and this time he looked a whole lot better. "Anne's going to be okay. Her spleen ruptured. That was where the bleeding was coming from so we removed it. Then we sewed her up hoping we can keep things quiet so the fetus has a chance to develop further."

"What? You did what?" I blurted out.

He explained that at seven and a half months, the fetus's lungs are still maturing and that in these traumatic situations, a pregnant woman's system produces a magic ingredient that accelerates lung development. "If we can just keep her from going into labor for thirty-six hours, the fetus should be viable."

"Holy shit," I said.

The doc got my drift, "I know, I've been practicing for forty-two years, and I've never seen anything like it. In fact, the whole hospital is back on its heels. The surgeons have never operated in a delivery room before. We had Ob nurses assisting surgery. But in spite of everything, I'm optimistic your wife will be fine and you will have a healthy child."

"We just have to get through the next day and a half."

"Yup," he said.

"Can I see her?"

"Of course, she's just coming out, so let's go."

My wife looks big when she's pregnant, but now she looked mountainous. "They tell me they trussed me up like a turkey. Want to see?" And before I had a chance, she tossed down the bedclothes to reveal her belly.

I almost fainted. Six rubber tubes stretched across her stomach.

"From looking at your face, I can tell that's it for bikinis," she said, a wan smile breaking across her face.

"How are you feeling?"

"Shitty, but that's a lot better than dead." Anne gingerly touched her abdomen. "And the baby's going to be okay, at least that's what they tell me. How are you?"

I took her hand, "I'll be fine. I'm just glad you're okay."

"I love you. Thanks for rushing me to the emergency room. They tell me we made it in the nick of time. Another couple minutes and I could have bled out."

I could feel my knees going weak.

"You look like you need to sit down," Anne said. I guess my face wasn't hiding anything.

We talked for a few minutes, then she sent me home to take care of the kids, telling me she'd be fine and dictating a laundry list of chores for me to do. When women start making lists, you know they're going to be okay.

And here's the kicker. Two days later, Anne delivered a healthy baby boy, naturally! She had survived a spleenectomy, and, with a network of rubber-covered wires holding her incision together, she managed to push out an infant weighing just a skosh more than a bag of sugar with a set of lungs that that would eventually carry him through a distinguished athletic career. When she walked out four days later carrying Vandy in her arms, many of the staff gathered to cheer for her.

Two days later, when I found myself in the emergency room with chest pains, I thought I was having a heart attack. The attending physician checked me out and said, "You're okay. Been under some stress lately?"

I told him what had happened, and he said, "I thought so. You're just hyperventilating." He picked up an ordinary brown paper bag, shook it open and said, "Breathe into this if it happens again."

So Anne walks out of the hospital with sutures from here to there and a new baby boy. And me, I come out with a brown paper bag. Guess who's the wuss in this family?

Finally John's assistant calls me, and I run down to his office to pick up the notes. I don't even wait until I get to the parking lot to read them. Walking down the stairs from his office, I rip open the envelope and breathe a huge sigh of relief. Instead of tearing my outline to bits, John's beginning to ladle out compliments.

John Grisham _____ 25 Feb 05 _____

Tony:

     You're getting very close. The overall story is working well. The hero and main characters are taking shape. The basic plot is in place. The setting is easy.   The subplots are being refined and discarded.

Finally some progress! He likes the story, hero, and main characters, the plot is coming along, the backgrounds to the action work for him. Am I on solid ground again?

     Since I like the basic plot, allow me to point out the obvious soft spots, and also to nitpick:

   1.   I wouldn't start with the face of Al Qaeda. Since Bin Laden is the greatest bad guy since Hitler, you don't need to overplay the danger.

        A thought - What is more terrifying than the face of Bin Laden? A sleeper cell here in the U.S. - something close to home. Al Qaeda in our backyard.

I thought he'd like Bin Laden but wow! An al-Qaeda sleeper cell right here in the United States—now there's a great spooky idea. And a much more effective way of introducing the bad guys.

     What if ------   You open with our hero Howie doing his lecture at UVA. He mentions his website and all. Then we see a college student at, say, Georgetown or Penn, looking at the website. The student is an Arab, and as it turns out he's the leader of al Al Qaeda cell. Much more about him later.

That'll work. I can do that! Make him a regular guy on the outside but a committed terrorist on the inside. The more people accept him and like him, the freakier it will be for the reader when they find out what he's up to—just like John's senior partner at the law firm in Memphis in *The Firm* who seems like an upstanding citizen until he starts talking about killing cops. I must remember that subtlety is needed here, not a sledgehammer approach!

2.   Act One is strong - it holds together well and will get the story off to a rapid start.   Watch, though, things like "using a homeless man as the bait to snatch Risstup." This sounds easy, but it's hard to pull off and make believable.

3.   Act Two ----

Why rent rooms in a nursing home? Can you do this? Why not just pick a low budget hotel?

Watch the scuba stuff. I used to dive, though I've forgotten everything. I think depth gauges are as automatic as tanks. Why would they use European stuff? They're not from Europe. They wouldn't sneak the gear into the country. You can buy it by the truckload at Dick's Sporting Goods.

Act One works for him—okay! So I'll take John's word for it about the homeless guy and find another way for them to get him out of there. Good point about the nursing home. A cheap hotel is better. And he's right about the scuba equipment. Why not have the terrorists purchase it here?

Back to our student and his sleeper cell - you could use him learning to dive, perhaps in a college class. Maybe he has a girl friend who get suspicious. He's a good Muslim and all, but he is in America. Maybe he likes beer and online porno. Remember how several of the 911 hijackers spent their last few days drinking and watching porno, quite contrary to their rigid religious beliefs.

He's not a slouch though. He's very committed, and he's not alone. He could be the suicide diver. There are copies

of Skin Diver magazine around his apartment. He watches
re runs of that old Lloyd Bridges TV show.

This guy could be a great character - he lives here, goes to
school, makes good grades, seems normal, puts up with the
post 911 resentments, and quietly seethes with hatred for
the U.S. And on and on.

John's sketch of the student and sleeper cell is terrific!
Thank you, John Grisham.

4.   Act Three ------

The computer stuff will be crucial, and it's here that Howie
can show off how smart he is.

WARNING - If Howie is able to piece together Risstup's
last flight using a stolen computer and working in a
rented room, why couldn't the Pentagon do it years ago?????

This is a potential hole-in-the-plot!. And it's important to make
the point early and often that the Pentagon has been asleep for
50 years, the cover-up is stale, etc.

I've got work to do here. Duh, if Howie can figure it
out using a laptop, with all their resources, why wouldn't the
Pentagon have put two and two together a long time ago and
resolved the situation before it spun out of control?

The Pentagon is just now waking up because of the Al Qaeda
threat, and they're such a bunch of bumbling idiots who are
more concerned with the political infighting . . . . .

You have to make sure the reader understands the basics of this
bomb. Most are as ignorant as me and will have a hard time
believing that a bomb that's been underwater for 50 years
can still be detonated and wipe out millions. You can start
laying this groundwork in chapter one.

It's too cozy for Howie's old friend to now be the Secretary
of Homeland Security.

Okay, so I need to get across the mechanics of the bomb
better. I'll really go to school on this. Somehow build a

convincing case that the nuke still poses a threat, oh, and by the way, work in the Homeland Security guy more believably.

> I'm not sold on the idea of Howie doing the actual diving and being able to find the bomb himself. Let's joust over this verbally.

I'm sure there's a way around this. Probably a stretch to have him recover the nuke. Anyway, we'll talk about it.

> Act Three needs some work, though the structure is there. Howie inadvertently leads Al Qaeda, M-11, and the good guys all to the Chesapeake Bay for a final showdown. Of course the good guys win. But maybe Howie is not happy. Maybe he threatens to go public with what has been an extremely covert rescue operation. Maybe the story ends with Howie in the Oval Office getting promises from the Prez that all the sleeping dogs will be found and destroyed.
>
> 5. The title: I like "Sleeping Dogs" much better, but keep working on it.

Okay, okay, I'm with you, John. I've been thinking of Howie using his knowledge as leverage, yes! But maybe there's another ending I can come up with that somehow makes Howie the hero. And my alternate title, *Lucky Once*, isn't playing for him yet.

> 6. Time is crucial here. This is a story that can take place in less than a month, maybe less than 2 weeks. You've got a man - Risstup- who's been kidnapped, or at least taken away. This situation cannot go on for long. The ticking clock is a great tool. "Three Days Of The Condor" is such a great movie, and one reason is that it takes place in about three days. I deliberately modeled "The Pelican Brief" after it, and that story covers seven days. "Marathon Man" is another example of great suspense over a few days, in a big city.
>
> This has the same feel

Comparisons to *Three Days of the Condor* or *The Pelican Brief?* Wow, I'll take those kinds of compliments any old time. And I better go back and read them both again. Got to make sure I keep that ticking clock tool working. Then I read John's final comment . . .

I'd like to see one more outline, more of a revision than something new. 3 page max.
Then it's time to start the chapter outline.

Wait a minute, did I read that right? He wants me to do a revision instead of starting from scratch! Yippee, after three and a half months I'm closing in on it.

But what's this business about a chapter outline? Another set of outlines? Another three months before I can start on the novel?

I think of the old joke about the Hollywood producer who hires a writer to do a screenplay. Rejecting the first draft, he tells the writer he needs to work on the characterizations. Then the producer turns down the second version, telling the writer to increase the plot tension. Work on dramatic impact, the producer suggests. Add a love interest. This goes on for months, with draft after draft rejected until the totally exasperated writer finally hands in his sixth one, and the producer takes the manuscript and glibly tells him, "Good, now I'll read it."

A chapter outline? *What the fuck?* John never said anything about a chapter outline. I will have written the damn book before I start it.

But then I remember what John said at our first lunch, "The last ten percent's the hardest."

CHAPTER 5

The Last 10 Percent

I dive into my sixth outline, making sure every detail is as tight and clear as I can make it. I finish it and drop it off with John's assistant.

In the middle of March John and I have another lunch. We start out talking about PEC, the Piedmont Environmental Council, an enviro group I volunteer for and John and his wife have championed. Founded thirty-five years ago by a prescient group of landowners concerned about sprawl radiating out from D.C. into the Piedmont of Virginia, the original members included heavy hitters like John Warner (who went on to marry Elizabeth Taylor and become a senator from Virginia), Forrest Mars (his dad invented a couple candy bars), and Paul Mellon (need I say more?). We're giant slayers, a fearless band of conservationists unafraid to take on the governor, the power company, Walmart, or Walt Disney.

The PEC sent Michael Eisner and Mickey Mouse packing when they tried to start a history theme park in our area. Eisner and company brought their influence to bear on the governor and legislature and thought they had a clear shot at turning the sleepy central Virginia city of Fredericksburg into a new Orlando with their history-park version of Disney World.

Shutting Eisner and Disney down impressed the hell out of John, and when I joined the board, he and his wife stepped up and supported us, not only to permanently protect their farm, but also to generously back our other projects. Now I've become a vice chair of PEC and I'm pretty active. It's a ball I bounce when I'm not sitting in front of a computer screen writing outlines for Grisham.

I take a few minutes to update John on the PEC projects we're working on, and when I wrap up, the spotlight's on him. I'm dying to hear what he has to say. He doesn't disappoint.

"The outline's good enough to go on," John tells me. I have to keep myself from leaping out of my chair.

He gives me the lowdown on chapter outlines. "They can be paragraphs and usually get tighter as you go along because at the outset you can't tell exactly where the book is going to go. As you move through the manuscript you keep revising your chapter outline. What you do is eliminate characters, add or subtract subplots, but your main challenge, Tony, is going to be to condense—with your hyperactive imagination you don't want to end up with seven hundred pages."

It's clear John can sense I'm getting antsy to begin the novel, and his closing comment is, "Take a month doing it."

Cooling my jets, I start working. If I thought crafting an outline was challenging, doing a chapter outline is even more daunting. An outline only has to sketch out the plot, but this new version adds the time sequence, so you have to literally decide day by day what's happening. And I'm not actually writing the novel; I'm describing what's going on from a distance, like a landscape artist painting an out-door scene indoors while staring at a blank wall. It feels alien, weird, even more off-putting than crafting an outline. Particularly bizarre when I transition from one chapter to another since there's this blank space that pops up between the two. Like Alice tumbling down the rabbit hole. Light goes out, pfft! TV picture goes black.

Blank space, oh wow, I'm thinking, as an incident from my ad days suddenly shoulders its way into my brain.

I flash back to a conference room on the ninety-some-thing floor of the Sears Tower where I'm presenting a major new campaign. Sears had hired my firm to broaden and soften its image from a purveyor of tires, tools, and batter-ies to a full-line department store with desirable brands of clothing, shoes, and sportswear. Customers had always val-ued Sears's hard goods, but most wouldn't be caught dead wearing anything with the store's label. The perception was brought to life by the adage about the guy who goes into Sears to buy a chainsaw and a suit. The guy tells the clerk, "Wrap the suit. I'll carry the chainsaw."

So I'm showing storyboards for a campaign of jazzy TV commercials starring celebs like Arnold Palmer and Cheryl Tiegs to a group of Sears honchos. The room's packed, and

I have the audience in the palm of my hand. These guys are used to seeing demonstrations of DieHard batteries starting a pickup at 40 below in the middle of the Artic. My spots are bouncy and high-spirited with catchy music tracks. The storyboards are large black cards with panes of colorful illustrations that depict the various scenes of the commercial. I point to each frame then adroitly shuffle to the next board. Having done this hundreds of times, I'm a pro at making cardboard come alive.

Their heads are nodding, their toes are tapping, and everyone in the room is appreciating how these commercials will jumpstart soft goods sales. Until the guy in the front row raises his hand. I know he's a biggie, the only guy in the top tier of Sears execs from the founding family. I'm thinking, *Oh shit, this guy's going to tell me this doesn't feel like Sears advertising and torpedo the whole campaign.*

"Tony, let me ask you a question . . ."

"Certainly," I say as I wait for the swish of the sword as it comes down on the campaign's neck.

The exec stands up and walks up to the easel. Pointing at the blank space between the illustrated rectangles, he asks, "What happens here? I've been looking at these things for twenty-five years and I've never understood what goes on in this space."

I want to say, *Are you kidding me? That's frigging cardboard, dude!* But I have a mortgage and kids heading off to college so I calmly explain, "These storyboards are just approximations of what the finished film will look like, so that represents a scene change, going from this frame of the commercial to the next, just like a cut in film."

"Oh, thanks," the guy says, and goes back to his seat looking as relieved as if I'd just given him a one-sentence encapsulation of the Theory of Relativity.

What business did this guy have sitting in heavy-duty presentations when he had no idea what the blank space between the storyboard panes was? About as much business as I have writing a chapter outline according to John's instructions and being baffled by the same spaces.

Yet I forge on, building the outline chapter by chapter. I figure that when I actually write the novel, I'll come up with some connective tissue to bridge these spaces if necessary. Or, as I explained to the Sears guy, the transition will be like a cut in film. Stairstepping through the plot, in the back of my mind I'm starting to think, *If I can ever I get this done to John's satisfaction, writing the novel will be a breeze. All I'll be doing is expanding the chapter outline.*

Yeah, right.

On April 14, almost six months after John's offer to mentor me, he gives me the go-ahead. With the approved chapter outline as my guide, I jump into writing *Sleeping Dogs.* Though Grisham might get five pages on a good day, even with four hours a day at the keyboard I barely get three, sometimes only two. At that rate, I figure it will take me three plus months to finish, with revisions pushing into August. I circle August 15, 2005, as my target date.

Not only do I have to write the first draft, but I have tons of research to do as well. I've never had to do much delving or fact-finding since my other books came out of my head. My first was a Hunter Thompson-style take on advertising, kind of a "mad men on parade" that received a deflating comment from a top-tier literary agent a friend set me up with. She scribbled on the manuscript, "Tony, I'm not sure anyone cares what you have to say." Stake through the heart, but at least I got my peeves with the ad biz out of my system.

I decided the world needed more funny novels, so I did one about a couple of women in their eighties who escape from an assisted-living center and go off on a series of madcap adventures (think *Thelma and Louise* for the geriatric crowd). That novel got me a young agent in D.C. who thought it was terrific. He even told me the writing was so hot he could almost feel the heat through the title page. Writers are suckers for compliments like that.

He peddles it around to editors and comes up with a bunch of "fixes"—i.e., editorial comments that he thinks can make the manuscript more saleable. I spend months doing the revisions, and he spends months shopping it around. After a year and a half with no takers, we call it quits, and I start on another comic novel called *Ads for God*.

Ads for God was hilarious, if I do say so myself. God contacts an over-the-hill ad guy and commissions him to do a campaign to improve his image. Of course, God turns out to be like any other client, full of nitpicks and bizarre critiques. My agent tells me he's not comfortable with the title and strongly suggests I change it to *God, Inc.*

We were vacationing with the Grishams in Venice when John got a call from David Gernert as we strolled over one of the canals. I could tell David was apologizing for interrupting his vacation as John abruptly said, "That's okay. What is it?" John listened for a few seconds, then tersely said to David, "Tell them to go take a flying you-know-what" and quickly hung up. "These guys have a million stores and sell a ton of my books," John harrumphed. "But I don't know where they get off thinking they can ask me to change a title."

But I'm not Grisham, so to keep my agent enthused I change the title to *God, Inc.*, and he starts submitting it to editors in New York. After a couple months, the word from the Big Apple is, "Comic novels are a tough sell. What's funny to one reader isn't to another." Editor after editor passes. My agent suggests more revisions, but it doesn't help. Another novel down the tubes.

So I try one last comic novel called *Say Something Funny*, and I'm about to send it off to my agent when Grisham offers to set me up with his agent, David Gernert. David's willing to give it a read, but to keep things on the up and up he asks that I end my relationship with my agent.

I FedEx the manuscript to Gernert. But then I don't hear anything from him for a couple of months. Is no news good news? Finally, I get a call from a junior agent at his shop who tells me he was totally blown away by my ending, and he's going to get my book in front of David. Weeks go by. One morning I get an email from Gernert apologizing for taking so long and asking if I'm still interested in having his shop consider it. What am I supposed to say?

He promises to get back to me by the end of the week. On Friday he tells me the good news and for a short weekend I'm elated. Then on Monday he calls and drops the bomb. "I'm passing on it, Tony."

Having been around the block too many times with comic novels, I decide to go with the flow, so I turn to popular fiction and crank out what I think is a barnburner. Takes me eight months and I ship it off to Gernert. Comes back with a handwritten note saying, "Tony, this doesn't work for us, sorry."

I'm wondering whether I should hang up my laptop and call it quits. On the wall of my studio I have a quote from Churchill: "Success is going from failure to failure with enthusiasm." But Winston never says how many failures you can go through before your positive outlook falters. And as Nora Ephron says, the only thing failure teaches you is that you can fail again.

That's when John makes his offer to mentor me, and after six months of outlines, I'm back in the novel-writing business, working on the first draft in the morning and researching in the afternoon. My shelves are crammed with works on CIA code names and B-52 design and construction. I learn the difference between hydrogen and atomic bombs and the mechanics of both. Start to get an idea about how the terrorists can come up with a mechanism to deal with the nuke's disintegrating TNT charge. I read stuff like Lawrence Wright's *The Looming Tower* about al-Qaeda and the pathway to 9/11, *The Complete Idiot's Guide to the CIA*, and a similar one on the Pentagon, plus a book John suggests on skin divers exploring a shipwreck off the New Jersey coast. I pick up *Chatter* on global eavesdropping and *In the Rose Garden of the Martyrs* and *Imperial Hubris* on the war on terror, cramming every corner of my brain with background information so I can write authoritatively.

Taking a deep breath, I lay out the first chapter, all the while keeping the objectives John has outlined firmly in mind: Make Howie likeable. Don't hyperventilate. Stick to the basic plot. I've absorbed so much of John's advice and words of caution that I now feel I have an internal compass to keep me on track.

I start out Chapter 1 by introducing Howie as he walks across the campus of his alma mater to give his lost nukes presentation to a friend's class four days before Thanksgiving. Memories of his glory days at UVa are kindled by this familiar setting:

> Howie Collyer pauses halfway across the Lawn, stopping to look down at the well-worn flagstone path so familiar to him from his college days as bits and pieces of memories from the distant past elbow their way into his mind. Bonfires blazed up and down the long, grassy courtyard as the ragtag halftime band played the school's fight song and the team carried him into the victory celebration on their shoulders.
>
> He glances down at the walkway, up at the arching elms for a few moments, then lets his

eyes wander down along the columned portico toward the magnificent Rotunda at the far end of the Lawn.

He recalls the rollicking cheerleaders in their white flannels and sweaters silhouetted against the roaring fires as they did cartwheels and back flips, bouncing up and down then scrambling to retrieve their megaphones to lead the crowd in the school's victory song, a thousand voices from across the grounds joining in, arms tossed over each other's shoulders, drinks splashing everywhere as they swayed back and forth in unison to the familiar refrain sung to the tune of "Auld Lang Syne." "We come from old Virginia, where all is bright and gay, let's all join hands and give a yell for dear old UVa!"

He was the most unlikely hero and his kick was a miraculous fluke. But having had only a handful of victories in the past ten years, to the students at the University of Virginia this win was as sweet as they come. And they all knew they had one member of the team, Howie Collyer, to thank for it.

Next, as John suggests in his notes, I write about Howie lecturing the class about the lost nukes. Since I've already made him a football hero, I don't need to worry about geeking Howie up with his computer wizardry. He sets up his laptop and projector with the help of a comely coed named

Bridget and proceeds to wake up the sleepy undergrads with his riveting lost nukes PowerPoint:

"The bombers refuel over the Mediterranean, the Atlantic, or the Arctic before turning around and returning to the States—each B-52 having at least one nuke in its bomb bay, some two, many three and four. Thousands of nuclear weapons in the air 24/7—as you guys like to say."

Bridget's hand shoots up in the air. "Were all these bombs armed?" she asks, her voice tinged with disbelief.

"They had to be, Bridget, because they were our main defense against a Russian attack. Having planes in the air at all times with armed nukes guaranteed we would be able to strike back immediately. Think of these B-52s as loaded guns, cocked and ready to fire."

"So they were flying armed nuclear weapons over the United States?"

"Yes, B-52s took off from all these bases around the country," Howie says, dialing down the volume as green dots flash on the screen showing the scores of Air Force bases to which B-52s were assigned. "And flew missions over the continental United States, across the Atlantic . . ." The screen above Howie's head again comes alive with thousands of flight patterns tracing across the country and threading out over the ocean.

A student wildly waves his hand, blurting out his question before Howie can point to him. "If there were that many planes in the air at all times as you show, weren't there some accidents? I mean couldn't one or two of these planes have gone down somewhere with nukes on board?"

"A bomber with a nuke crashed in North Africa." Howie's video zooms into the Moroccan base to show the burning aircraft. "One of our planes disappeared somewhere over the Mediterranean with two bombs aboard. We dropped two off the coast of British Columbia and had a scary accident in England where a plane went off the runway and crashed into a building housing three nukes."

The student sitting next to Bridget sneers, "British Columbia is close enough. I certainly hope they didn't drop any in the United States."

Howie winds up and says in his most understated but impending tone of voice, "I wish they hadn't."

"You're not going to tell us there are nuclear weapons lying around the United States?" Bridget is perched on the edge of her chair, her eyes bulging.

"I'm afraid so, here's where a bomber came apart in mid-air and we dropped a couple of nukes on a farm in North Carolina. One in Georgia, two in the drink off New Jersey."

"How come all this was never made public? How could they sweep all this under the rug?" Now she's on her feet with her hands planted on her hips.

"The Air Force claimed these were training missions with no armed nukes aboard. And you have to remember there was no Internet back then, no CNN—only three networks with the news tightly controlled by the Pentagon. This was at the height of the Cold War with the Russian nuclear menace on everyone's mind."

Howie brings up a slide. "Here are the eleven unrecovered nuclear weapons reputable sources believe are scattered around the United States. Go on the Web and check for yourself. It's all out there. In fact, I urge you to check out my website—sleepingdogs.us."

The room is dead quiet.

"This is where I need your help. No one in Washington will pay attention to this problem. It happened on someone else's watch almost a half century ago. Many of the generals and admirals in the Pentagon were in diapers when these accidents happened. That's why my website is named sleepingdogs. That's the Pentagon's approach: Let sleeping dogs lie. I tried for ten years to get them to pay attention to the threat. And didn't do my career any favors as a result."

I love the diaper line, and the whole sleeping dogs thing ties everything together. I'm pumped about the progress I'm making—the first chapter is humming along. John's brainstorm about having Howie bring the lost bombs story to life in a UVa lecture is working beautifully. And I've dressed it up with the elaborate video presentation and the students' reactions so it's almost like the scene is right out of a movie.

Writing with Grisham reminds me of painting by numbers. I expand and animate one of his knockout ideas and then move on to the next, assembling them to create an amazing story.

After establishing Howie's character and getting the reader up to speed about the lost nukes, it's time to put in the hook as John directed. Readers know there are bombs out there, now I need to shock them with the info that the most evil force in the world is aware of their existence.

I set the next scene in an apartment on the campus of Rutgers University, where a foreign exchange student named Mehran is living with a spoiled little rich girl named Melanie, who's always whining about her boyfriend not spending enough time with her.

"But I thought you were the big scuba diver. How can you resist?" Melanie knows that anything to do with diving fascinates Mehran, and she regularly tries to use his interest to entice him to take trips with her. Melanie is always picking up the dive magazines littering Mehran's room, goes diving with him at the college's pool, and often takes him out to a quarry a couple of hours away to practice.

"So then you have to do a favor for me, Mehran," Melanie says, running her hands inside his shirt, letting her fingers ripple over Mehran's tight and trim stomach muscles.

"I must do my work right now."

"Are you sure? I have another idea . . ." Melanie says suggestively, her hands sliding under his waistband.

"I have at least five hours' worth of work to do, honestly."

"It's not nice to say no to Melanie," she coos.

"I'm sorry. I do my best work when I'm alone."

"Then how about ten o'clock? Is that too early?" she asks.

"I will be ready at ten. I promise."

"I'll pick you up at ten then—but you better be ready to party," Melanie says, shaking her finger at him. "Bye," she says, blowing him a kiss as she walks out the door.

Mehran waits until he hears her footsteps on the stairs before he goes into his bedroom, locks the door, and turns on his computer. The link to the website is obscure, deliberately disguised behind a series of other websites so no one accessing his computer would accidentally stumble over it. As he clicks on the links to the site, he reflects on his good fortune. An American is doing all his work for him, peeling back the layers of secrecy to open up the nation's best-kept nuclear secrets to anyone with the curiosity to undertake a search.

So astounding, these Americans. So dedicated to freedom that they make aircraft fully loaded with thousands of gallons of aviation fuel available to a few men with passion, commitment, a few penknives, and boxcutters so they can turn the planes into guided missiles and bring down two of the Great Satan's tallest buildings.

One last link and he would be there. There it is, Mehran thinks as the opening page of the website flashes on the screen.

My next chapter sets up the old pilot who might know where the bomb was jettisoned forty years ago. First, I introduce the VA hospital doctor, Tom Knowles, who's snapped some disturbing photos of patients in a special secret ward, the "Annex Three" John spitballed at our lunch. I'm beginning to paint the picture of a highly classified government program to secretly quarantine people in a VA hospital ward they don't want talking. Kind of a domestic Guantanamo thing. With all the crazy renditions and CIA skullduggery going on, readers will buy in and accept that Risstup, the pilot, is held there as well.

I decide to have Knowles share the snaps with his wife, Lucy, and spill the beans about what he thinks is happening one evening at home over drinks:

> "I don't know who they are, CIA, Navy Seals, Rangers—they are all dressed in civilian clothes. Jeans, sport shirts, sneakers, real ordinary stuff yet there's nothing ordinary about what they are carrying. These guys are all armed to the teeth. Uzis, big fat Glock revolvers. I even saw one with grenades on a bandoleer under his coat. It's like they're members of some private army. And you don't want to mess with them. You can tell they'd just as soon shoot you as say hello. Very freaky."

> Settling back on the sofa, Tom slides his arm behind Lucy's back and takes a sip of champagne. "If you think that's bizarre, get this. There's this one guy who must be over eighty. And he's American, I'm certain. C'mon, this guy belongs in a nursing home somewhere in Dubuque, not in this place. There's no paperwork on him, nothing. It just doesn't make sense."

> "So what's he doing in there?"

"That's what I've been trying to find out. Then a couple days ago, he starts telling me something about his aircraft being involved in a crash."

"He was a pilot?"

"I guess. And then this afternoon I was talking with him. I mean, you don't converse with him, he's out of it. But he starts mumbling something about a bomb."

"What?"

"As near as I can figure, his plane accidentally dropped a bomb. He becomes very agitated about it. This afternoon, I stopped off to see him just before I came home. And he grabbed my arm and he said, 'Dr. Knowles,' and this is the first time he's said my name, 'you have to help me find the bomb.'"

As Howie and his family enjoy Thanksgiving dinner at home in the next chapter, I introduce his wife and children. One of his daughters is a character who tells a funny story about a local car wash where the female attendants jump inside the cars and do more than clean the interiors. At his wife's request, Howie doesn't bring up his obsession with lost nukes until an alarming call from a doctor at a VA hospital interrupts dinner.

Bright and early the next morning, Howie hustles up to Pittsburgh. As he's driving, he thinks back to his Pentagon days and recalls a shadowy government agency called "Vector Seven" that was rumored to be responsible for covering up everything having to do with any nuclear mishaps. My research tells me there are all kinds of what are called "black programs" at the Pentagon, top secret projects that are so classified that very few people even at the top echelons know they exist. With bizarre names like "Broken Spear" and "Echo Orange," they have elaborate codes to keep the unauthorized from logging in. It's not too far-fetched to imagine that some of the black programs were set up so long ago and had so few participants that their existence is now forgotten. It's the guise I need to concoct a nasty underground secret effort to make the world safe for nukes, not unlike the Mafia law firm in Memphis that provided John with the bad guys for *The Firm.*

So I begin to fill in the blanks for the reader about the nefarious agency that's been able to stymie Howie and keep the whole lost nukes issue under the table. Howie begins to put two and two together, guessing that they might be connected to what's going on at the VA hospital.

He thinks back over the doctor's call. *Is it possible the government could keep an Air Force pilot under wraps for almost fifty years? Or is the pilot just beginning to come out of some kind of amnesia? All I know is that if the pilot has anything to do with a lost nuke, you can be sure the government would make sure he is hidden away somewhere.*

Howie's cell phone rings. He checks the screen and doesn't recognize the number but since the call is from the Pittsburgh area code, he quickly answers it.

"Mr. Collyer?" The voice on the other end is female and disturbed, still in control but edging toward frantic. "I found your number on Dr. Knowles's desk. I'm a nurse at the VA hospital. I know this is a stab in the dark, but Dr. Knowles has disappeared. You know who he is, Knowles?"

"Yes, as a matter of fact. I'm driving up to meet with him right now."

"Forget about that. He's gone, disappeared. His wife is worried sick. Knowles left an order to administer a drug to one of our patients—an older man. It's a dose that might very well kill him. When I checked with the supervisor on duty, he said if I didn't administer the injection, he would find somebody else to do it."

Collyer checks the screen on his direction finder. "I'm two hours away. Put that order in your pocket and get the hell out of there."

I can feel the novel picking up steam. Al-Qaeda's been introduced, the reader's drawn in, and now I'm injecting exciting incidents, fueling interest, feeding the fire. Glancing up to the top of my screen, I see it's time for lunch. I leave Howie, the nurse, and Knowles, put my computer to sleep, pack the dogs into the Gator, and head back down the lane to our house two hundred yards away. We'd always wanted to live in Keswick, the foxhunting country on the Richmond side of town where Anne's mom grew up and her parents settled after they retired. But nothing was available when we relocated from Chicago, so we ended up buying a fifty-acre farm named Fielding (a historic property that was originally part of the homestead where Meriwether Lewis was born and raised) on the west side of Charlottesville. I delighted in walking through the same woods and fields where the legendary explorer hunted and trapped two hundred years before.

Five years later, when someone made an out-of-the-blue offer for Fielding, we jumped at the chance finally to live in Keswick and bought a horse farm with an existing house and cottage, a couple of barns, and an ideal building site toward the back. For two years we lived in the front house while we built our dream home and my writing studio on the hill overlooking it.

We've put the farm in conservation easement to help our neighbors keep the area looking much the way it did when Jefferson rode his horse down from Monticello to call on friends. He loved the countryside and named it "the Eden of America" for its gently rolling hills covered with a patchwork of woods and pastures knitted together with whitewashed three-board wooden fences and dotted with horses and cattle. It's a special part of the country that seems to attract those who appreciate both splendid vistas and a remarkable way of life. This is a place where the guy who repairs tractors, the garbage lady, and the guy who mows lawns for a living are accorded the same status as billionaires and celebrities.

"There are no secrets in Keswick," the local historian likes to say, and bumper stickers read, "Drive slowly and enjoy the view on Routes 231 and 22." Landowners take great pride in Keswick's appearance by manicuring their road frontage, keeping their fields mowed and their fences sparkling white.

So moving to Keswick was like coming home for us. Since my mother-in-law, Ellie, had deep roots in the community, Anne and I were immediately accepted.

In addition, since Anne's godmother is Anne Barnes, who'd grown up with Ellie at Cloverfields and is a Jefferson descendant who reigns as the grande dame of Keswick, we are all accorded privileged status. Which, for a Yankee carpetbagger like me, is big stuff.

Anne Barnes presides like royalty over social gatherings at Cloverfields, sitting in a chair in the parlor while friends line up to pay homage. And if Anne is queen, Ellie is first lady.

Often she sits alongside Anne Barnes at parties, and the two white-haired octogenarians tag-team, regaling their audience with stories of life at Cloverfields. Tales of the old South that hark back to a simpler, gentler time.

Like the dinner where Ellie's sister remarked about the entrée served at a dinner party on the farm, breaded and deep-fried slices of a mystery meat served on a bed of lettuce, "This is so delicious, what is it, veal cutlet?"

"No, Phillipa dear," the hostess answered, "what you are enjoying is what we call Rocky Mountain Oysters." Ellie and Anne milk the story for all it's worth, describing the change in Phillipa's expression as it dawns on her what she's eating.

Ellie continues, "Like a cloud coming over the sun, she went absolutely gray, and for a minute I thought she was going to toss her cookies."

"And if there was any doubt in her mind, Coles took care of that," Anne adds, teeing it up perfectly for Ellie. Coles is the host, a devilish and spirited character.

Ellie delivers the punch line perfectly, "So Coles spears one with his fork, holds it up in her face and trumpets, "Bulls' balls, Phillipa girl, you're eating bulls' balls."

Pulling into the driveway in my Gator, I see Anne's car sitting in the garage. If she happens to be home and through with the art project she's working on, we'll enjoy lunch together, a pleasant change from the fast track back in Chicago where the cynical credo was, "In sickness and in health, but never for lunch."

Though I'm eager to share my delight with the progress on *Sleeping Dogs*, I know I can easily bore her to death when I sound like a nine-year-old kid who comes home from a movie and breathlessly relates the entire plot in exhausting detail. But when I'm spending that much time on my novel, it's hard not to bring home a few things from the office. And she's always gracious enough to ask, "How did it go today?"

"Great, another fifty pages in just under a month. I think that's pretty good progress," I answer her.

"I'm glad for you. That's terrific. But take your time with it. No point in rushing. Remember what John said."

She's right of course, there's no clock ticking—except in my own head. Patience has never been my strong suit. I have trouble carrying on a phone conversation lasting more than a few minutes, absolutely dread conference calls, hate meetings so much I designed the conference rooms in our agency with glass walls so I would be pleasantly distracted by eye-catching young account execs, writers, and art directors passing by. I'm always incurring Anne's wrath by barging ahead at dinner parties, sneaking food off my plate before everyone is served.

So when it comes to talking about writing I have to set my cruise control at 55 mph and severely curb my enthusiasm. Friends know I'm a writer and often ask out of politeness and curiosity how my book is going. If I say, "Fine, it's working well, thanks," that usually suffices. When I succumb to the urge to prattle on about lost nukes, al-Qaeda, and Howie Collyer, eyes begin to glaze over, and people start to look around for an easy exit.

John's good about touching base with me about the novel. Renée even inquires about it from time to time when we get together. "How's the writing going?" they'll ask over dinner. And as much as I'd like to give them every last detail, I resist and say, "Great. Having fun with it. Thanks for asking."

It's much more enjoyable to talk about John's books, as he always has an incredible tale about spending time on death row with an inmate who recounts the murderous spree that landed him in the slammer, or an industrial polluter in Mississippi he's turning into the antagonist of his latest legal thriller.

So I bottle up my excitement and instead carry on endless conversations with myself while I'm bush hogging on my tractor, chainsawing firewood, or mulching gardens. My imagination's working double and triple overtime. I scribble glimmers of ideas and inspirations that come to me at all hours of the day and night on stacks of yellow stickies, which I have to harvest regularly from all over the house.

Writers are notorious for being distracted and self-absorbed. If you have daughters or sons, tell them never to marry one because they'll end up playing second fiddle to some plot that's wormed its way into the writer's brain until it's taken over every cell and clogged up each synapse, rendering the writer speechless and glassy-eyed for a good part of the day. There are times, with plot details and character ideas swirling around in my head, when I've missed a turn and driven ten miles down the wrong road, begun a conversation only to have my brain short out, or started a chore only to stop transfixed and dumbfounded halfway through, my mind sputtering, "Now what the hell was I trying to do?"

I'm in my ideal element perched on my riding mower cutting grass. I can let the characters and dialog completely invade my thoughts and still manage to make the turn at the end of the row. Only problem is I have run out of gas once or twice.

For a spouse, being married to a writer is a special curse. "What in God's name are you doing?" my wife will say as she sits up in bed at three in the morning, rubbing her eyes and blinking at the light coming from my side of the bed.

"Oh, you know, just jotting down an idea so I don't forget it."

"Uhhh," she groans as she collapses back into the covers.

The next morning, I read the sticky that's stuck to my night table and see the name I had found in the phone book but forgotten until my three o'clock inspiration. "Sharon Thorsen—nurse. Yesss!"

Later, I'm back up in the studio starting the scene where Howie meets Sharon for the first time. I've sketched most of it out in my sleep, so it assembles easily.

Glancing back at her, Howie walks to the counter and places his order. Sparkling blue eyes, long brown hair, nice figure from what he can tell. But obviously distraught. Fidgeting with her purse, anxiously looking around the shop, her eyes regularly darting to the front window.

"So what's going down?" Howie says as he sets the coffee in front of her.

"Are we safe here?" Her voice is shaky.

"I can only guess . . ." Howie wasn't going to get into details about Vector Seven. Did they know he was in Pittsburgh with Thorsen? Had they tapped her phone? No way of knowing.

"Let's just assume we're a couple steps ahead of them," Howie says.

"Who's 'them'?"

Forty-five minutes and two rounds of coffee later, Sharon Thorsen is a new woman. Steamed up over the treatment of her patient and the disappearance of Knowles, infuriated by the thought that the government would stash terrorists in a VA hospital, and stunned that the Pentagon would cover up the fact that there are live nukes scattered around the United States—not to mention ordering the assassination of an elderly veteran— Sharon Thorsen sees there is only one option left. She checks her watch.

"If we move fast, I think I can get him out of there."

While Thorsen returns to the hospital to snatch Risstup, Howie borrows a computer (this is before smartphones) from a student sitting next to him at Starbucks and emails his wife and old college buddy Winn Straub, who is a top guy at the CIA. Howie's letting his wife know he won't be home for a while and trying to get Straub to find out if it's Vector Seven that's running the cover-up at the VA hospital.

Using Straub's CIA perspective, I sketch out the intelligence apparatus for the reader and talk about black operations, the organizations that are deep under cover at Langley, and other intelligence agencies that execute secret missions.

Straub receives Howie's email and suspects his buddy might be back to chasing lost nukes:

Winn hoped that retirement would mellow Howie, but as he reads the email, he realizes Howie's back to being his old self.

It's an open secret that the Pentagon and CIA are stashing terrorist suspects anywhere they can hide them. Restricted by the courts, hounded by the media, and with Congress threatening investigations, the suspects and prisoners are the Pentagon's hot potatoes. Anyone going anywhere near the subject finds the temperature quickly rising.

Why is Howie getting involved? What interest could he have in a VA hospital where they are concealing Pentagon prisoners? Straub asks himself as he rereads Howie's email.

For the past six years, his former roommate has been a broken record on the subject of unrecovered nuclear weapons. Straub had watched as Howie turned from a backslapping former jock to a moody and confrontational zealot who badgered Pentagon generals on the subject of lost nukes until they cut him off at the knees.

Straub pours himself a cup of coffee and carries the laptop over to the island.

"Howie," he begins typing, "what the hell are you doing messing with some Pentagon special program? If you thought you got under their skin with your lost nukes, wait until you see what they do to you on this. Get back to Charlottesville and bury your nose in a good book, play some golf, take that nice wife of yours out to dinner. Enjoy life and keep yourself out of trouble."

He types in a link to a more secure email server for Howie—only Straub and the agents under his control have access to that server. Straub figures, *The least I can do is try to keep Howie out of their line of fire for a while.*

I'm cooking on all burners now. Not only do I have an old buddy nicely ensconced at the top levels of the CIA to aid and abet Howie, but I can use Straub to add perspective and interpret what the Pentagon is doing.

I write a dramatic scene where Sharon kidnaps Risstup from the VA hospital by stabbing a guard in the neck with a syringe full of sedative in order to make her escape. Then I wake up the Vector Seven people at the Pentagon with the news that one of their detainees has been kidnapped.

The novel's clicking along, with the various intelligence agencies teaming up to confront the threat of a lost nuke falling into the wrong hands. To help the reader understand why Vector Seven is so concerned, I introduce General Watt, who's the Pentagon's point person on lost nukes, plus Lester Revelt, the civilian who's the real power behind the nuclear weapons industry.

Watt's heavily lidded eyes are the first to see the email from Pittsburgh. He shakes his head as he rereads it. How could they have discovered the identity of the batty old Air Force officer? Watt checks his watch. Almost 1600 hours.

His phone buzzes.

"General Watt," he answers. Then quickly, "Yes, sir, I have seen the email."

Within Vector Seven, Lester Revelt, the chairman of Tecnor, a multibillion-dollar defense contractor, commands immediate respect. Technor runs the bomb-production facilities at Oak Ridge and recently took over the operation at Los Alamos for the Pentagon and the Department of Energy. A PhD and astute businessman, Revelt's word is law in the nuclear weapons establishment; he has a private line to the Secretary of Defense, his own security force, and a fleet of jets and helicopters.

"Watt, I want you to devote all of your attention to this matter. If someone gets that loony old bird singing it could be hell to pay."

Fleeing the VA hospital and Pittsburgh in a cab and now holed up in a fleabag motel in Lancaster, Pennsylvania, Howie Collyer and Sharon Thorsen work with the pilot to help him recall where he ditched the bomb. I'm now in the middle section of the novel John sketched out for me in which Howie's going to use all his computer tricks to fill in the blanks in the aviator's mind at the same time as al-Qaeda and the Pentagon are turning the world upside down looking for them.

While that's going on, I have the Vector Seven black-ops people confront Howie's wife and daughter in Charlottesville about Howie's whereabouts. Any intel agency worth its salt that suspected Collyer would go after his family. So I create a female agent named Patty to question Sylvie and Grace Collyer.

"Look, Ms. Collyer," her voice sounds soft and sincere but Grace immediately senses a current of sarcasm underneath. "It has been determined that Howard Collyer is engaging in activity contrary to the security of the United States of America. Do you understand, Grace?"

Grace is surprised at the mention of her first name.

"Now you can either help your father by giving us some information, or . . ."

"I think we should help, Grace. I really do," Sylvie says.

"That's the spirit, Sylvie," Patty says, smiling for the first time. "I like your attitude." Grace is rattled by how much they know about them.

"Mother, shut up. Just shut up," she mutters, hoping she can stall for time.

"I am my mother's attorney. You direct your questions to me," Grace insists, but she wonders how long Sylvie will hold up.

"Your mother seems to understand the trouble her husband is in. And she seems willing to help."

"I repeat. I cannot allow you to ask her questions."

Patty ducks around Grace and quickly shoots a question before Grace can react. "Did your father take a phone call from a VA hospital on Thanksgiving evening?"

"Mother, don't . . ." Grace pleads.

Before Grace can stifle her, Sylvie wails, "I told him not to go! I told him that call was big trouble!"

Patty turns to her boss. He smiles and nods.

"Thank you, Mrs. Collyer," Patty says, leaning over Grace to speak directly to Sylvie. "That's all we needed to know. Appreciate your help, folks. You both have a great day." Patty whirls and heads off across the driveway towards the waiting SUVs.

A lot of novel writing is housekeeping, paying attention to detail to make sure you don't consternate or baffle the reader. In film production, a script supervisor keeps the director from going astray by jotting down elaborate notes so that a character doesn't have a red hat on in one scene and a black one in the next, or start with a half-empty glass of beer and end up with a full one in the following scene.

Fiction writers don't have that luxury, and since they are dreaming everything up, they have to stay on their toes. Not just with details, but with character consistency, plot turns and twists—any loose end can derail a reader. That's why

I had to deal with the fact that an organization like Vector Seven is going to chase down Collyer's relatives, and eventually I'm going to have Winn Straub bring them in.

Then there are timing issues to keep the plot cooking. The pilot can't reveal the location of the bomb too early, or my novel will, as John has warned, peter out. So stuff has to happen in the motel room while Howie and Sharon are working with Risstup to uncover his secret.

I use the email from Straub telling Howie to back off in order to create tension between Howie and Sharon. Reading it, she freaks and begs Howie to knock off his dangerous quest. Howie comes back at her hot and heavy. The scene also enables me to knit in a loose end involving Howie's wife and kids. What's he doing about them? And then at the end, in what I think is a deft piece of writing, I find a way to have the pilot come out of his trance for the first time.

> Howie takes another tack. "Okay, so we give up! Let's leave the major right here. Pin a note on him saying, 'Please return to VA hospital and resume injections of atropine'? Is that what we do? And you go back to the VA hospital like nothing happened? How are you going to feel when you walk into that crazy ward and find out the major died the night before?"
>
> Sharon sits down. Howie senses he's finally getting through.
>
> "But the fact that your wife has been threatened—doesn't that mean anything to you?"

"Look, I care deeply about my family. But consider the future of the whole human race."

"Isn't that a bit dramatic?"

"Hell, no. If we leave hydrogen bombs scattered around our country, how can we tell Iran or North Korea or any of the nations who are close to developing nuclear weapons to act responsibly? How can we put pressure on the Russians to secure their unrecovered nukes? Otherwise, sometime, somewhere, someone will make a fatal mistake and another accident will occur that will make Chernobyl look like a fender bender."

Howie goes on, "Look, I know this is no picnic. But when they are backed up against the wall, they make mistakes. Look how they mishandled Risstup. Hid him in a ward full of terrorists so he stuck out like a sore thumb, then had to order his execution when they were threatened with his memory coming back."

"And now we're the threat."

"We have been from the beginning. The minute you made that call to me on my cell phone you became part of it."

"What about your family?"

"I'm going to email Winn, tell him we're sticking with it, and ask for his help with them. He'll protect them. So you in?"

Sharon nods. She nods reluctantly, but she nods.

"Good," Howie says as he reaches for his laptop. "So we're sticking with it."

They are both stunned by the next thing they hear. Neither one has heard a word out of Risstup since they took him out of the ward three days ago. But there was no mistaking what Major Risstup said or to whom it was directed.

"That's good," Risstup says, his voice creaky but resolute. "Because I hate quitters."

While Collyer and Sharon continue to work with Risstup, it's time to bring the al-Qaeda operation to light. In order to understand how they have the capacity to track Collyer and ultimately recover a nuke, the reader needs to see them as resourceful, well-equipped, and absolutely ruthless, able to dispose of anyone who gets in their way. I've gone to school on al-Qaeda and read everything I can get my hands on about the organization. Instead of locating them in an expected place in the Middle East, I decide to set the al-Qaeda cell that's monitoring both Collyer and Mehran in a large Indonesian city. I'm trusting my readers to accept that Indonesia has a huge Muslim population, so it makes sense for al-Qaeda to have a presence there.

Hamil is the operative assigned to coordinate with Mehran in Pittsburgh and to track the American. Though he's temporarily lost contact with Collyer, he's confident he will soon surface. What Hamil learns the hard way is that the leader of the cell has lost confidence in *him*.

Hamil smiles. The ultimate irony is that the only group who would listen to Howard Collyer is America's most reviled enemy—al-Qaeda. While the Pentagon ridiculed Collyer and ran him out of the building, to al-Qaeda he is a saint and savior. Little does he know it, but if Howie Collyer manages to lead them to a nuke, his name will go down along with the other famous martyrs to the cause.

They have put an extensive network of cells and operatives in place. It is only a matter of time before someone locates him.

He's still staring at the screen when the door to the private office opens and El-Khadr steps out followed by the stranger who mysteriously showed up a half hour ago.

El-Khadr steers the stranger over to Hamil's computer station and says, "Hamil, I'd like you to meet your replacement."

Hamil does not understand. He stutters as he stands and shakes the visitor's hand. "Replacement? You said nothing about this. Where are you assigning me?"

"Far away," El-Khadr says. He quickly slips a Beretta out from under his robe, levels it at Hamil's forehead, and puts a bullet between his eyes. Hamil collapses like a puppet whose strings have been cut, his body slumping off to the side with a series of hollow thumps.

Stepping over Hamil's body, El-Khadr pulls out Hamil's chair and gestures to his replacement to sit down. The slender computer programmer kicks Hamil's feet out of the way and pulls himself up to the computer.

"Get to work, Muhsin," El-Khadr says, clapping him on the shoulder. "You have much to do—we're running out of time."

Back in D.C., Winn Straub decides that Howie's too pigheaded to back down and that it's time to shelter his wife and daughter, so he speeds down to Charlottesville to get them to a safe place. And as it turns out, it's just in the nick of time.

Three Suburbans doing ninety-five, windows blacked, their sirens wailing and filled with burly men wearing sunglasses, are racing down the Interstate in the opposite direction. Neither of the women chooses to remark on the three SUVs, but their heads slowly swivel to watch them as they fly past.

"I hope they don't tear my house apart," Sylvie finally says as the Suburbans disappear over a hill behind them. Grace says nothing. She realizes how lucky they are.

They stare out silently at the wooded banks of the Interstate zipping by for a few minutes. Then Sylvie reaches across the seat and puts her hand on her old friend's arm. "Now you can fill us in on the details. Did Howie take the pilot out of the VA hospital?"

Winn nods.

"And this pilot knows where a lost bomb is and Howie is bound and determined to recover it?"

Straub ducks his chin again.

"So who's after him?"

"Hard to say, exactly."

Grace pipes up from the back seat, "So who were those guys we just passed, then?"

"Look, ever since 9/11 there's been a lot of funny stuff going on."

The research I've been doing is turning up an unexpected gift, a treasure trove of information. In the rush to strengthen our intelligence capability after 9/11, Congress both created new agencies and beefed up the existing ones. But as so often happens in Washington, more doesn't always mean better. Turf battles abound, and instead of sharing intel, which was the problem revealed by the 9/11 tragedy, the tendency is for each agency to silo off its operations.

The more I read about the rivalry between the alphabet soup of intelligence agencies—DHS (Department of Homeland Security), CIA, DIA (Defense Intelligence Agency), DNI (Director of National Intelligence), NSA (National Security Agency), FBI—the more I realize that I can use that conflict to enrich and add credibility to my story.

With the exception of Winn Straub, who is staunchly on Howie's side, the rest are conniving bureaucrats misusing their power to advance their organizations' and their own personal ends. Not only can I take advantage of them to move my story along, I can also shed some light on the abuse of their positions of power and influence. The Crusader Rabbit in me comes out as I realize I can use *Sleeping Dogs* as a bully pulpit to inform my readers how the intelligence operations are spending as much time looking out for their own interests as they are protecting America from terrorists.

So as he takes Howie's wife and daughter to the CIA's base outside of Williamsburg, I have Straub continue to explain the situation.

"So who were they?" Grace insists.

"If I had to guess, most likely the Defense Department."

"Someone who doesn't want the bombs discovered."

"Exactly."

"But what gives them authority to act like this? It seems like they are almost a paramilitary force operating domestically," Grace asks.

Winn nods. "Nature abhors a vacuum, as you know. CIA has dropped the ball a bunch of times. We failed to predict both India and Pakistan's nuclear tests. Missed Saddam's invasion of Kuwait and failed dismally on 9/11. The Defense Department is taking up the slack by building a rival service to CIA—all in the name of fighting the 'war on terror.' They have their own spies, soldiers, weapons, budgets, ducking congressional oversight and shifting money around to fund covert actions, operating with complete impunity. Some Pentagon officials call what they are building 'the secret army of Northern Virginia.' I bet that's what those people who came to visit you were. Delta Force, Gray Fox, secret army—all the same thing."

It's summer in Virginia, and I'm on top of the world with a hot new novel coming bit by bit out of my computer. I can't wait to have Anne read my manuscript, which is 150 pages so far, and to finally get it into John's hands. I'm stringing pearls according to the Laws of Grisham with the secret army of Northern Virginia coming from the black programs that derive from the Pentagon's insistence to keep the unrecovered nukes off the radar. I've concocted a scary bunch of bad guys who are just as ready to pull the plug on their allies as stop terrorists.

And then, with al-Qaeda, I've created a set of really abominable characters who think nothing of putting a bullet in the brain of one of their colleagues. It's the nastiest group of villains imaginable, and they are all chasing one retired guy, a nurse, and a geriatric with the secret. I've got a best-seller going. I can feel it.

My imagination goes haywire. I daydream I'm on the set of the *Today* show chatting about what it's like to write a novel with John Grisham. Maybe John will join me? How big an advance will I get? Will there be a Porsche Turbo in the offing? Who's going to play Howie in the movie version of my book? Harrison Ford, maybe? Will I be asked to write the script? Big money in that.

Though we live comfortably, flying around in John's jet has given me a taste of what it's like to have big bucks. So nice to pull up to the back of a plane, toss your bags onto the tarmac, hop on, and take off. No crowds, no lines, no removing shoes. Just comfy seats, good friends, a glass or two of champagne, and Paris or Venice seven hours away.

Regaining my senses and coming back to earth, I realize I need the Pentagon to discover that al-Qaeda is also tracking Collyer, so I come up with a brilliant concept. Since al-Qaeda has lost Collyer's scent, they decide to send a flyer with Collyer's photo on it to an email list of American Muslims in the hope that someone will recognize him. Doctoring up his photo so he won't be recognized as Howie Collyer, they Photoshop a headscarf on him and write some copy about an abducted husband, pulling on Muslims' heartstrings with a sob story about his poor wife.

But the leaflet is intercepted by a smart young National Security Agency analyst, who sees past the Photoshopping and, when she erases the headscarf, recognizes Collyer. Circulating the handout with the revised photo throughout the intel community, it doesn't take long for Vector Seven and their operatives in the Pentagon to realize since the copy is in Arabic and the photo is of Collyer, there can only be one group that's tracking him.

And I stir the pot by getting more government agencies involved. The Secretary of Homeland Security, Lucien Jimmick, and his ace assistant, Doug Abel, as well as the Director of National Intelligence, Michael Prendergast—all are eager to find a chink in the Defense Department's armor, and they think Collyer and his search for the lost bomb could provide it.

"This is Tuesday," Prendergast says, checking his watch. "Collyer probably kidnapped the pilot sometime Friday night. That's almost four days—amazing he's lasted this long."

"I'd bet CIA is shielding him, his wife and daughter squirreled away at the agency's facility in Williamsburg," Jimmick, the DHS chief says.

"Why do you say that?"

"College roommate was Winston Straub, top echelon at the spook factory—been there thirty years."

"So you think Straub's running this on his own, not an agency priority?"

"Most likely. Unless they see the same potential you and I do."

Jimmick nods. Prendergast turns to look out the window. "It's a long shot," he says, sounding more hopeful than pessimistic. "If those Vector Seven people get to him, Howie Collyer is toast."

"And I hate to think of what would happen if al-Qaeda was on his trail and he found a lost nuke."

"That we have to avoid at all costs."

"Yeah, but if somehow we could stop al-Qaeda and let the Pentagon take the fall for putting the nation at peril. The blowback would be phenomenal. The Building would be reeling for a decade."

"We would get the credit and Collyer would be a national hero."

"Amazing, but I don't see a Hollywood ending in the cards. Too many people playing hardball out there. Any minute that phone could ring and we could hear that Collyer's been found floating face up in the Potomac. All of a sudden, the Pentagon's off the hook and we're shit out of luck."

Staring out the window, neither Jimmick nor Prendergast can think of a thing to say. It's a situation they hate but have been in many times—no choice but to wait and see what happens next.

CHAPTER 6

The Reckoning

On August 16, I finish up the novel with a stellar ending, only a day off schedule. Mehran, the suicide diver, gets blown out of the water before he can reach the bomb. The Defense Department takes the heat for sticking their heads in the sand, and Howie Collyer's not only vindicated, he becomes a national hero. I print out the 385 pages and proudly hand the manuscript to Anne.

"Take your time with it," I tell her, lying through my teeth as I'm dying to have her devour it in one sitting. But I'd learned the hard way that isn't going to happen. When you've been working on a novel for the better part of a year, reading and rereading page after page, you're dying for reactions. But to a reader, your three-inch-high stack of 8 ½″ x 11″ double-spaced pages isn't a soufflé to be enjoyed in a few bites, but to be read at a leisurely pace, thirty or forty pages at a time. I can count on a week, maybe ten days, before I get Anne's opinion.

Meanwhile, I have to resist every urge to ask, "How's it working for you?" or, "If you're not doing anything right now, how about picking up my book?"

For if I pester her, I know all too well what I'll get. If she's said it once about reading my manuscripts, she's said it twenty times. "Look, buster. For months you've been preoccupied with your novel and haven't given me the time of day. All I hear is *Sleeping Dogs* this and *Sleeping Dogs* that. And now that it's finished you're running in here every five minutes to check on my reaction, bugging me to read it. Cool it, okay? I'm going to take my own sweet time with it. And if you don't like that—tough!"

"You're right, sorry," I say, trying to relish the slice of humble pie that I've been served. As much as it kills me, I have to give her space.

So I watch silently as the stack of paper on the right side shrinks and the one on the left rises. I'm secretly gloating at all my literary accomplishments—the way I started off with Howie's kick that made him a legend; the way I bring to life his computer abilities; how I use the rivalry between the intelligence agencies to backdrop my story; the deft technique I used to introduce Mehran and al-Qaeda into the narrative. Anne's got to love it, and how could John not fall for it also?

A week goes by. Then two. I busy myself with PEC matters, sending off a bunch of emails to penny-pinchers in the legislature who are threatening the state tax credit for conserving land. Some developers hate land being taken out of commission by conservation easements, so they try to torpedo the tax credit program with their politician pals. We have to go to bat every year to remind the delegates and state senators that since agriculture and tourism are Virginia's two largest revenue producers, it only makes sense to encourage land conservation. Farmers can't grow crops in subdivisions, and people don't visit Virginia to see strip malls. Our state's program is the envy of the nation, but it's a never-ending battle to keep it going. All worth the effort when you gaze out at some of the vast vistas of fields and farms we've protected.

Now Anne's down to the last few pages. I hover in the hall and saunter through the doorway just as she turns the final page.

"So, what do you think?" I ask as she turns over the last sheet of paper.

"I saw you standing out there waiting for me to finish, you know." Fortunately, she's smiling. "It's good, it's very good," she says.

I want to say, *Just good?* but settle for, "So what works for you?"

"I don't know specifically. The whole thing plays nicely. You've done a terrific job with it. The characters work, you've got some exciting action, and it really is frightening that there are bombs out there that could be easily recovered."

"So tell me more," I ask, realizing I'm pushing. I'm dying for her to say, *Tony, you've written a killer novel. It's going right to the top of the charts.*

But instead I get a straight-arm, "What else do you want me to say? I've pretty much given you all my reactions."

"How about Howie? Is he likeable?"

"Tony," Anne says in her best cut-the-crap tone of voice, "Look, I told you. The whole thing is good. I'm not a critic. You've gotten all you can get out of me. What you need to do is give it to John."

I'm so pumped about the manuscript that I give it a quick once-over for typos, print out a fresh copy, and drop it off at John's office with a note that says, "John, Hope you like it. Appreciate all your help in making it work."

If I thought waiting for Anne's reaction was difficult, waiting for Grisham's is hell. Like after a big pitch in the ad biz when you're waiting for the thumbs' up or down, I'd go over every detail of the presentation with a microscope. Did I play that right? Did I handle the wrap-up deftly? Was the advertising too edgy for the prospective client? Or not edgy enough?

What's so confounding is that all the backing and filling, the questioning, the second-guessing, is a total waste. It's all water over the dam. There's not a damn thing you can do to affect the outcome. And though you're fully aware of your own ability to influence the outcome, you keep agonizing anyway. It's an exquisite form of self-flagellation reserved for artists and anyone who chooses to put his ideas on the table.

Eight days later, John's assistant calls. "Tony, John asked me to tell you your manuscript's ready. You can pick it up anytime." *Unsettling that John didn't call*, I'm thinking. He could have phoned and said, "It's terrific, Tony, just a few odds and ends here and there you need to work on. But it's really close. Take a look and we'll talk." But he didn't call. His secretary, Bert, did.

I park in the lot across from his office and push the button for Oakwood Books. John leased space downtown when he outgrew his writing cabin on the farm. After Anne and I won the Met Home award, John and Renée asked us to design it for them, and we did a knockout job. All stainless and plastic, gleaming oak floors, custom furniture, subtle but very snazzy. Bert buzzes me in and I take the stairs in twos. Open the door and walk across the front hall to her cubby.

"Hi, Tony. Here you go," she says, handing me the cardboard box containing my manuscript. *Uh oh*.

Her expression tells me she might as well be handing me a box of ashes straight from the crematorium. There's an envelope taped to it.

"Is John around?" I ask, looking past her to the door to his office. It's closed.

"Yes, but he's busy."

Bad vibes, I'm getting bad vibes. *Bert looks like someone close to her just died, and John is too busy to see me. Oh, shit.* But I'm such a basket case I don't trust my reaction. Hell, she could just be having a bad day, and after all, John is a busy guy. *Maybe he loved it?*

"Well, thanks. Tell John I said hello," I say, mustering as much cheer as possible.

"I'll do that. Bye."

This is not the way I had it scripted, I think as I head out of the building toward the parking lot. I expected John to come out of his office with a big smile on his face, clap me on the back and say wonderful things about my manuscript. Instead I'm getting the cold shoulder. I pull the car door shut, open the envelope, unfold the sheaf of pages, and read:

---

john grisham   23 aug 05
_____   _____

Tony:

Here's the book back, with some notes. I did a lot of scribbling
on the text, then decided to put together my edits, which I've
crudely broken down into two groups - big ones and others. Give
this all a good read, then we'll talk.

Big Edits:

     1.   **First Draft**: It's a mistake to submit a first draft.
Maybe a second or third, but never the first. This reads like a
hurriedly thrown together effort with no time spent reading and rereading what was written. There are too many mistakes - wrong
names, multiple use of the same word in a sentence, misuse of
small facts, and so on. Dialog must be repeated out loud several
times before it's finished; it's the only way I know to make it
sound real.

          Many of the mistakes are small and easily fixable, but
taken as a whole they slow down the reading and become frustrating.

My first inclination is to fight back. "Hurriedly thrown together effort." *What's he talking about? I spent more than five months on it.* "No time spent reading and rereading . . ." *I must have read and reread the damn thing fifty times.* Dialog doesn't sound real . . . *Okay, okay, I can work on that.* "Easily fixable . . ." *Of course, after all, it is a first draft. This isn't so bad, or is it?* I read on.

     2.   **The Plot**: This is story about an old pilot leading Howie
who's leading Al Queda who's leading the clowns at the Pentagon to
the site of a ditched nuke. This is the basic plot.

          But the first half of the book has virtually nothing from
the pilot - he's kidnapped and sits drooling in a wheelchair in a
cheap motel for several days while subplots pop up everywhere. If
Risstup is talking, we don't know it, and since it's the main plot,
it should be on stage.

```
        The focus of the first 200 pages is the intelligence wars
in Washington.   There are too many bad guys.   Too much backdrop,
exposition, explaining, politics, and, worst of all, sermons.  Some
of the soapbox spills absolutely stop the action cold.
```

Ouch, that hurts. People don't pay good money to read about drooling. And the subplots business—I thought I was brilliant bringing the intelligence wars in.

I quickly leaf through the four more pages of his notes. I'm thinking, *An extended beating with a rubber hose would be more fun.*

```
        3.   Howie:  He comes across as a likeable character, which is
crucial, but a few things are trouble:   (1) he seems much too
unconcerned about the danger his family is in; (2) it's hard to
believe that one kick would make him famous for generations of UVA
fans, though we all know they've had little to remember over the
decades; (3) his old Pentagon stuff is repeated over and over and
over; once he's a hi-tech wizard in high demand, then he's a
babbling  fool  screaming  in  the  hallways,  and  screaming  and
screaming.
```

John gives me a compliment with one hand and takes it away with the other. Howie's likeable, but then he's a babbling fool screaming in the hallways, and screaming and screaming. And he's not concerned about the danger his family's in. *Wait a minute! Is Grisham off base on this? I was sure I got across that Howie was concerned. How much of this stuff can I argue about with John? I don't want to piss him off, but on the other hand I don't want to roll over if I don't agree with him. But, wait, there's more.*

```
        (4) And Howie does some dumb things - sits in a Starbucks
for hours when he should be worried about being watched; lays up in
the same cheap motel for days, following the exact same routine,
begging to get noticed by someone; doesn't change cabs after they
flee Lancaster and he suspects the driver might be a bad guy.
Howie is looking over his shoulder, or should be.  He would think
hard about his movements, his trail.  A Cub Scout could follow
Howie.
```

Zowee! Apart from the stinging I'm feeling, the harder part is my growing realization that John's right. *Howie wouldn't sit in a Starbucks or hang out in the same motel for days. He's not a stupid guy. He should know better than that. Why did I not see these problems? What was I thinking?*

It's no wonder that when I picked up the manuscript Bert looked like she was sitting shiva and John was hiding in his office. What was he supposed to say to me? "You really blew it, Tony. This is a total piece of crap, with mistakes and bad writing from top to bottom"? *Better that I swallow the pill and come to grips with it on my own.* I read on with a creeping sense of doom.

```
     4.   VA Hospital: (1) Why are the terrorists there?  They add
nothing to the story - it's not about the war on terror, it's about
finding a lost nuke.  They blast onto the scene early in the book,
and you keep waiting for an explanation.  If the aim is to make the
government look bad, there's way too much of that already in the
story.
     And the fact that the terrorists and Risstup are in the
same ward?  It's another unnecessary subplot that weighs down the
real story.

     (2)   The idea that the terrorists are delivered by heavily
armed goons is bizarre.  Why would they want the attention?

     (3)   I don't know if the terrorists play a role later in the
book - I only finished the first 200 pages - but, frankly,  since
they had nothing to do with the plot during the first half of the
book then they should be eliminated.

     5.   Goon Squads:   These goons dressed in black and roaming
the country in black suburbans make cartoons out of the scenes.
They kidnap Knowles,  haul in terrorists to the VA hospital,
intimidate Collyer's family, barge into a woman's house and steal
her computer, race from DC at 95 mph to "arrest" Sylvie and Grace,
and on and on.  They're evil but not stupid; surely they've had
good training.  They would not roam about doing everything possible
to attract attention.  And their flagrant disregard for basic
constitutional rights is over the top.

     Subtlety is needed here, not a sledgehammer approach.
```

He only finished the first 200 pages? My manuscript is so awful he couldn't even get through the last 150? And then he hits me with the "sledgehammer approach"—talk about a wicked uppercut! I'm scrambling around my emotional machinery trying to find some equilibrium. *Is he right about everything? Cartoons? Goons? Morons? Over the top? Did I screw this up that badly?*

C'mon, Tony, you're not even through page two. Face it, you've got a total debacle here, I tell myself.

> 6. **Bad Guys:** There are too many, and too much time is spent setting them up, getting them on stage. Aside from the goons, these people (Abel) do not have police authority and cannot go around flashing badges and intimidating law abiding citizens.
>
> Virtually everybody who works for the government is either an idiot or just plain bad. The voice of the narrator is so slanted it loses credibility.

Is there anything he likes in this draft? Anything? Ten years of writing novels and I'm nowhere. I can't even put a first draft together. *Ninety percent there*—my ass. *Talk about a sinking feeling.* Not to mention having subjected John to the thankless and onerous task of slogging through my pages of sloppy and cartoonish writing, lack of subtlety, narrator without credibility, profusion of subplots.

I'm feeling guilty, inadequate, scared, disappointed, and just plain old bummed out—all at the same time. Yet, I read on.

> 6. **Mehran:** The idea of this character is good, and necessary, but there are some big problems. (1) On page 24 we are told exactly what he, and Al Queda, have planned for the rest of the book. This is a fatal mistake! Remember the old adage - **Show, don't tell!**
>
> (2) Every potential reader knows that Al Queda is bad, so don't spend much time re-inforcing this. Mehran's inner thoughts are unnecessary. He's a terrorist (though it's a mistake to mention Al Queda so early - let the reader guess or start to assume - subtlety!) - and he's involved with a much larger group that is planning something evil. Gradually give the reader background on Mehran and his activities. By Chapter 2 we know what he's doing, who he's working for, and their ultimate goal.

> (3)   We know what happened on 9/11 - we lost, they won - don't beat this into the story.
>
> (4)   I know these guys prey on stupid white girls who like to screw and can't get laid, but Melanie is almost too good to be true.   Would her parents - any parents - so wholeheartedly endorse such a relationship with an Iranian misfit - provide scuba trips for him, send the jet, and allow her to blow thousands of $$ on a whim??   It's too easy; make it harder; show some guile and sacrifice on her part, and his.   And when we later talk about Thorsen, and Grace and Sylvie, the women in this story start looking like morons.
>
> 7.   **Thorsen:**   On one hand, she is very smart and savvy.   On the other she quickly tosses aside her career, safety, friends, family, whatever, to help Howie, a guy she just met, kidnap Risstup and risk imminent death.   Tough sell.
>
> 8.   **Knowles:**   He's kidnapped rather dramatically on page 46, then never seen, at least by page 210.   Days go by without Lucy reporting his disappearance to the locals.   No press, nothing. Think about reality - a local doctor is missing for more than three days - and you've got tv crews in the driveway.
>
> > An idea: Forget Knowles, he just complicates matters. Let Thorsen be in the one who gets close to Risstup, maybe she secretly cuts back on his brainkillers, he starts to talk, she gets alarmed and quietly contacts Howie.   Nothing happens at the Pentagon until someone wakes up and notices that Al Q is watching Howie.   By then they have Risstup, who's talking, not drooling. Thorsen is more believable because she's emotionally attached to the old guy.

Subtlety, tough sell, women look like morons, think about reality—how much worse can it get? I'm looking at a total rewrite. This draft is so bad maybe I should just junk it and start over.

Or maybe there's a bright side? I'm a glass-half-full kind of guy by nature, had to be to endure almost twenty years in advertising. Say John's right with all his critiques. If I can fix everything, I'll really have a strong novel. So I need to get over all the painful reactions, catalog everything that's a problem, and take the time to fix it. *Only two more pages left. Hang in there, Tony.*

9. **Risstup:**   (1) At some point, early in the story, everybody starts talking about, and accepting as fact, that Risstup has blabbed about a lost nuke that he ditched, and that he can lead Howie to it. But the readers don't see this!! All we hear from Risstup is ". . I don't like quitters."

(2) The assumption - Collyer's kidnapped an old pilot who'll lead him to a lost nuke - becomes established fact early in the story, long before Howie and Risstup start talking.

(3) Place yourself in the motel room for four days with a kidnap victim who's been brain dead for 50 years. Something has to happen! What are they doing in there for 16 hours a day?

(4) It doesn't ring true - shorten the motel stuff considerably - Risstup has to talk early so the plot can move along.

10. **Vector 11:** Very confusing about how much or how little they know about Risstup, but the obvious question cries for an answer: If they are so worried about Risstup, and so willing to kill anybody who stands in the way of nuclear glory, why wouldn't they just knock him off years ago? They've kept him brain dead for 50 years. Why run the risk?

11. **The Soapbox:** Get off it. Forget your own political views. Stop slamming every character who works for the government.

6. **Delta Force:** I know nothing about these guys, but is this a project that would involve them? This must be accurate. Also, you're much too harsh on DF. These guys can't brag about their successes. Again, the bias against everybody in Washington takes away credibility.

7. **Lancaster:** College towns are great settings, especially a place you know well. But for Watt and the bad guys to look at a map and decide that Howie is in Lancaster just because Thorsen went to school there is too much of a stretch.

8. **Grace and Sylvie:** Grace could be a great character, but when she wilts before the goons on the porch you want to scream. Sylvie starts off as a likeable counterweight to her husband, but is reduced to an imbecile.

9. **Title:** I like Sleeping Dogs a thousand times more than Lucky Once.

There are a lot of notes on the pages, so I won't belabor the points here.

The most important point is one that needs to be made without being filtered through the complexities of friendship. So, set that aside. The best advice is based on brutal honesty. This book, at least the first half of it, has so many distracting subplots that the main story takes a back seat. The basic plot exists in concept, but it doesn't make it to the page. Most of the time is wasted weaving backroom plots and conspiracies that add little to the real story.

Slow down. Take your time. Stop preaching. Listen to real dialog. Repeat out loud every thing you write.

```
        I'll read the next draft, but not if it's ready in six weeks.
   I spent hours on these pages, and I'm not complaining.  But I can't
   do it again for several months.

        Write the next draft, then read it carefully, more than once.
   Give yourself a year to re-write, re-polish, re-work everything
   until the mistakes are gone and the story moves along.
```

I'm sitting in my car holding John's notes, staring out at the parking lot. My cell phone rings. It's Anne. She knew I was going to pick up the manuscript.

"Did you get John's reactions?"

"Yeah."

"Well?"

"We'll talk when I get home."

"Tell me what he said."

"It's not good."

"How bad?"

"You don't want to hear."

"C'mon, Tony, that's why I called you."

"Okay, he said it was sledgehammer writing, a lack of subtlety, too many subplots, the women come across as morons and imbeciles . . . and that's just for starters."

"He didn't like anything?"

"Not a damn thing I can see."

"Come on home. Let me read it, and we'll talk."

"Okay, okay," is all I can muster. "See you in a few."

CHAPTER 7

Picking up the Pieces

When you get to age sixty, you'd think you would have developed a grounded and rock-solid psyche tempered and toughened by life's rough and tumble. Instead it takes me two days and not a few glasses of wine to get to the point that whenever I pick up John's notes I no longer feel the psychological equivalent of dry heaves.

Paralysis and self-pity are my appetizer and main course with sides of bewilderment and humiliation. Apart from the shock of being totally blindsided, the bitterest reality is confronting the multiple errors I made in spinning out the plot and developing the characters.

There's a moment when I shout out to myself, "Screw it! Who needs this crap!" and imagine myself tossing handfuls of the manuscript into a raging bonfire. *Why should I bring more pain and disappointment down upon myself? Haven't I had enough already?*

Anne is no help. "Look, you go from the bush leagues to the majors and you're surprised you're getting thrown out?" she offers. Or, equally consoling to someone who's wallowing in a vat of rarefied emotional excrement. "When you think about it, you're damn lucky John backstopped you. Otherwise you would have ended up with another book no one would buy."

Sitting back with a cigar gazing out at the fields and the mountains beyond, I reflect that I've discovered the fourth Grisham Law of crafting a bestseller—just because you think you know the first three laws doesn't mean you're going to be able to make them work.

Not until a couple of days later that I begin to get my bearings and face up to leafing through the manuscript to read John's notes. While his critique felt like a full-blown carpet-bombing, his jottings in the margins are grenades rolling under my writing chair, each one indisputable proof of my ineptitude and lack of attention to detail.

Afterward, he will go back to the dorm and make love to Melanie, the one homely member of Sigma Nu who has given him the cover to infiltrate into the heart of America. Without her, he would be another skinny and nerdy foreign student, grinding away at his courses, snubbed by the majority of the students, left to eat alone at the dining hall and sit off to the side at classes and in the library, ostracized by his skin color and thick hair as inferior being.

As he is deciding which of the other two choices to make, he hears a snarling whisper coming from behind the row of wide and stately elms lining the walkway.

isn't Sigma Nu a fraternity?

Ouch! Sigma Nu is a fraternity. Nice job, Tony.

He thinks back over the doctor's call. *Is it possible the government could keep an Air Force pilot under wraps for almost fifty years? Or is the pilot just beginning to come out of some kind of amnesia? That's one of the first things I'll ask. All I know is that if the pilot has anything to do with a lost nuke, you can be sure the government would make sure he is hidden away somewhere. Hell, it's possible they've even forgotten about him. Inadvertently mixed him in with a bunch of suspected terrorists. God knows, they've certainly done things like that before.* *not believable*

Two screwups in one paragraph! Repetitions I should have caught, not to mention writing with a total lack of credibility.

An hour later, a hundred miles south in Charlottesville, Virginia, Sylvie and her daughter Grace are sitting in the kitchen drinking their second cup of coffee. Sylvie has been a nervous wreck ever since Howie left for Pittsburgh. Grace quickly made some calls, moving appointments around so she could stay with her mother for a few days. Not that she thought her father was in any trouble, but her mother was worried sick. Yesterday they visited Howie's parents in the nursing home on the other side of town. Grace thought it would be a good distraction. But the visit has only added to her mother's anxiety.

"I thought they looked well," Sylvie Collyer says to her daughter Grace as they rehash the visit to Heritage Hills. "But they both seemed upset Howie didn't visit."

And twenty pages later, I do it again! *Uggh!* . . .

"I don't care about the money but I'd appreciate it if you'd give me a little advance notice next time, that's all. My parents would kill me if they knew I was skipping class."

"I will try to do that." Mehran went on Jeffri's Garden early that morning and the message was clear: all gardeners in zone 6 should start to prepare to dig up their dahlias

isn't it Sunday?

I can't even keep the days of the week straight. I say it's Sunday then have Mehran talk about skipping class.

And I write that the windows of the government goons' Suburban are blacked out and then have Howie's wife noticing the guys are wearing black sunglasses. "How can she tell?" John asks.

repeat

> Jimmick has been looking for a way to partner up with the DNI, anything he could do to curry a little favor with the new DNI would be to his advantage. And if he could find a chink in the Pentagon's armor, find some aspect of national security he could turn to their advantage, both he and the DNI could make political hay with it.

And here's another repeat, this time it's a new record, three in a paragraph!

wouldn't he keep a much lower profile?

> away is a godsend. The crew at the Mug N'Muffin has American diner food down cold. And the working stiffs of Lancaster flock to the diner for its burgers, hoagies, French fries and coffee that as one patron described to Howie, "makes your ears perk right up." The seven takeouts Howie's ordered have made him a fixture in the last couple days and Howie's generous tips have turned him into a favorite customer.
>
> But Howie's forgotten about the shift change at the flooring factory. Five men and two women are already lined up in front of him—a good ten-minute wait.

Of course he would keep a lower profile. He's trying to avoid al-Qaeda and the Pentagon.

NO —

❶ NO one would ever trust the goons.

> Before Grace can stifle her, Sylvie wails, "I told him not to go, I told him that call was big trouble."
>
> Patty turns to her boss. He smiles and nods.
>
> "Thank you, Mrs. Collyer," Patty says, leaning over Grace to speak directly to Sylvie. "That's all we needed to know. Appreciate your help, folks, you both have a great day." Patty whirls and heads off across the driveway leaving Grace and Sylvie standing at the front door watching the group as they head toward the Suburbans. Grace feels Sylvie start to edge past her through the door, she grabs her arm to restrain her.
>
> "I have to find out about Howie, Grace, please let me go!" Her mother bursts into

abrupt ending

I make Sylvie a moron, turn the Vector Seven people into goons, and add an abrupt ending to boot! Now I start my sermons while Mehran is diving in a quarry.

helicopter to occupy visiting divers. As he propels himself deeper, Mehran can feel himself entering another world. Not only the world of the deep, but the world of salvation. The world from which he will present his gift to the people of the United States--the world in which he will perform his ultimate calling, serving the greater glory of Allah by detonating a nuclear weapon that will reduce the East Coast of the United States to ashes.

WAY TOO MUCH PLOT –

Underwater, though it is still American water, the vileness of the perverted American culture recedes, all its sick materialism, the worship of the dollar, the Sodom and Gomorrah-like pursuit of personal pleasures, pornography, gluttony, professional sports, a Las Vegas of sin and excess dedicated to preserving the abhorred Zionists.

SERMON

SHOW, DON'T TELL

Mehran feels the rage building in him as he swims to sixty feet and glides over the rusting hulk of the hook and ladder. *Invading Iraq was the last straw, it would be the nail*

wouldn't he concentrate on his diving

"I've been telling you that all along—there are risks. But we have an opportunity to change the way the government deals with nuclear weapons, shed some light on the scary policies they are pursuing and end this whole nuclear charade."

Bad sermon

"And you would risk your family's safety for that?"

"I'm not convinced my family has anything to do with this." *?*

Not only am I standing on my soapbox, but I've also created a poorly crafted statement for Howie. He has to be more concerned about the danger he's putting his family in. He can't just blow off Sharon's question with something like, "I'm not convinced my family has anything to do with this." What in the world was I thinking?

Then Grisham nails me with the ultimate understatement. For the first time in the three days since they've taken him from the VA hospital, I have Risstup speak, uttering the phrase, "I hate quitters." John suggests another response: "Might he not ask where the hell he is and who are the two people in the motel room?" What I've written is so ridiculous he's got me chuckling.

And my most serious mistake is revealed. I continue to have the characters talk about Risstup's lost bomb when the old guy hasn't yet revealed it to anyone. As Grisham points out, I also bring up Knowles when I haven't talked about him for a hundred pages, and I make Sylvie look even more idiotic with each new scene.

> "It's all fitting together. The doctor who later disappeared from the ward, Dr. Knowles--the husband of the wife who I spoke to--he put in a call to Collyer at home during Thanksgiving dinner. Collyer's wife guesses he found the number through Collyer's lost bombs website"
>
> "You got all this from a chambermaid?" Prendergast marvels.
>
> "It's amazing what you can do with a few good people. Anyway, the doctor told Collyer about the detainees held in a special ward of a VA hospital in Pittsburgh and specifically about a pilot who was regaining his memory about a bomb jettisoned during an airborne alert mission. Collyer's wife told our operative that despite her objections, Collyer hustled right up to the VA hospital the first thing Friday morning."
>
> Jimmick motions to his assistant, "In his visit to Pittsburgh yesterday, Doug Abel confirmed that the special ward is for real, the doctor has disappeared, the nurse is on temporary leave and nowhere to be found, and the pilot has vanished into thin air."

[Handwritten margin notes:] where is Knowles? what is his wife doing? when did Risstup say this? She's indeed a mom - will tell all everybody.

John underlines my major mistake again and again throughout the manuscript: How can everyone know he dropped a bomb when the pilot hasn't told anyone yet? *How could I have possibly done something so unbelievably mindless?*

I go back through it, and sure enough, there's page after page with dialog or exposition communicating that people know Risstup jettisoned it, yet Howie and Thorsen are sitting in the motel room waiting for him to reveal his secret. That's a screw-up of major proportions, and I've done it repeatedly.

But then suddenly, 170 pages into the manuscript, I discover six or seven paragraphs *without a criticism!* Howie's explaining the ins and outs of nuclear weapon design to

Sharon Thorsen. I'm getting the reader up to speed on all the details so they can understand what's going on. It's highly technical stuff that's a challenge to bring to life, and I'm amazed and delighted John likes it:

Nagasaki, that's inside the hydrogen bomb. The atomic bomb is ignited by a four-hundred pound charge of TNT. The TNT activates the fission process of the atomic bomb which creates the pressure and radiation to ignite the second stage of the bomb –the hydrogen bomb part."

"So far I'm with you."

"The early weapons were so powerful they had to be dropped by parachute so that the bomber didn't get caught in the mushroom cloud. The Pentagon's term for it was 'retarded delivery'. Some of them were designed with shock absorbing honeycomb noses."

"So they had soft landings."

"Yes, and these things were built like tanks. I mean the people who designed these bombs designed them to stay intact and not to fall apart."

"Even in water, or buried in mud?"

"From all the estimates I've heard, the casings of the bombs will stand up to salt water for another ten years at least. When seawater starts seeping in, yes, the TNT will be affected. That's what I think the government is up to. Hoping that they will stay sleeping for another ten years so by then they will have been degraded and rendered harmless."

"But in the meantime?"

"In the meantime, no one wants to take the chance of jostling one of these bombs and setting off the four hundred pounds of TNT. TNT is highly unstable. A dredge from a salvage tug could bump into a bomb accidentally, a line from a fishing trawler could scrape the bomb up against a ledge, use your imagination—anything could set the TNT off."

"Couldn't they retrieve them with divers? Divers who are precise and careful?"

"The Pentagon has studied that to death, believe me. And what they discovered only underlines the gravity of the situation. The chance that a nuke will break apart during recovery is too great. How would it look if we accidentally exploded one of our own bombs? Some diver attaches the cable at the wrong spot? It's murky down there and he can't see? The cable scrapes against the bomb casing, spark goes off inside and ignites the TNT? Once that goes, all hell breaks loose. Detonating one of our own nukes would make past Pentagon blunders like blowing up the Chinese embassy in Belgrade or

"Good stuff" is pretty high praise from a writer of John's caliber. And he's right: there's snappy dialogue, a concise and compelling explanation of the threat the bombs pose, and it's a real demonstration of the hours of research I've spent on the subject. On the other hand, it's only one out of hundreds of pages. One out of 385 to be exact, and that's a pretty lousy batting average.

Only once have I been steamrollered this badly, laid out flat with no way to get up. Another flashback to my ad days. The agency I worked for had just gone through a merger with two other ad giants, and though I made a wad in the deal, our chairman had given up my position along with the rest of the company.

No longer creative director, I now reported to one from one of the other agencies, an imperious blowhard whose claim to fame was a couple of award-winning Volkswagen commercials he'd written ages ago. With his finely honed Manhattan sensibility, he deemed that my Second City ad background automatically classified me as a second-rate creative talent. New York ad people derisively refer to Chicago as "Critter City" for all the Charlie the Tuna, Tony the Tiger, and Toucan Sam animated ad campaigns created there.

I knew my days were numbered, but I had one shot at saving my job—a pitch for the Minolta camera account. The chairman had back-channeled it my way, maybe out of guilt for selling off my job, maybe because he thought I could knock it out of the park. In any case, I put my best people on it and worked day and night to put together a world-class presentation.

A creative director's worst nightmare is facing a pitch with no ideas, nada, zip, nothing. For the first time in my career, the bad dream came true. There were bits and pieces, odds and ends of ideas, but no barnburner, no surefire hit. I kept sticking my head into offices saying, "So you got the big one yet?" to my teams, and all I saw were blank faces and slow-motion shakes of the head.

Facing an internal creative review in a couple days, I began to panic. I'd made my reputation and climbed up through the ranks as a creative manager, a person who could ride herd on a hundred plus copywriters and art directors and inspire them to come up with stellar concepts. But while I was a creative leader, master strategist, and consummate salesman, I wasn't an idea guy, so I was dependent on my troops. And for the first time in years, they were letting me down.

The creative review was a disaster, at least for me. As much as I tried to bluff and dance my way through, it was obvious I didn't have the stuff. My new boss, the creative director, was gloating at the fact that I had no killer ads, and to make matters worse the chairman decided that to fill the vacuum he'd come up with the recommended campaign himself, effectively elbowing me out of the way.

So my boss and the chairman put on the Minolta pitch and I sat in the back row, more spectator than participant. The fact that they didn't ace the presentation and win the account didn't matter. I was typed as a minor-league talent, and the handwriting was on the wall. Vanderwarker's career at that agency was in a nose dive; it was crash-and-burn time for Tony.

Yet as they were penning my obit, I made an incredible comeback. In a couple months, with some lucky breaks and a miracle or two, I landed on my feet with my own agency, and, for a total personal investment of 400 bucks, grew it into one of Chicago's top ten and escaped the ad biz before I was fifty with a pot of money, at least some hair left, and my health in good shape.

Failures are painful, but I've learned if you give yourself time, the hurt dissipates, like bubbles in a glass rising and popping.

With the manuscript, gradually I step over the shock and self-pity to where I can invoke the cliché "a learning experience" to characterize my plight. As Oscar Wilde aptly wrote, "Experience is the name everyone gives to his mistakes."

Because I'd written five novels, I thought I knew what I was doing. But John has written twenty *published* novels. So I'm playing tiddlywinks when I'm really in a game of five-card stud, way over my head. I thought I'd gotten John's laws down, but I hadn't internalized them, so they came to life in the writing. Plus, I'm already counting the money from the advance and taking my eye off the ball. Distracted and inexperienced is a nasty combination. That's John's point about it being a first draft. I wasn't minding the store, so I made simple mistakes I should have caught. And I was not experienced enough to catch the most egregious errors. A major wakeup call is what it is.

John said, "Slow down, take a year . . ." A year? Hell, it's the end of August now. It's been almost a year already. Does he really mean another twelve months? Okay, if that's what it takes, I'll devote the time to it. After all I've faced precarious situations before and survived. I can deal with this one. I need to get up, brush myself off, and move on.

Sorting through my past for solid ground, I think back to another case of distraction that nearly led to disaster for me. My boss had just given me the chance to do some ads for one of the largest accounts in the country—Anheuser Busch. And the pitch wasn't to be made to some low-level brand manager but to the chairman himself, August Busch.

I stopped off at the bathroom a couple minutes before I was supposed to go on, totally distracted by my upcoming presentation to the chairman. I stepped into a stall, unzipped, and was about to let it rip when the bathroom door opened. What I heard next, to my absolute horror, were the voices of women merrily chatting as they came in for a mid-morning freshen-up.

No wonder I didn't see any urinals when I walked in. I'm in the damn ladies' room! I thought as I quickly flipped the lock on the door then jumped up on the toilet seat while I stuffed my junk back in and quietly zipped up. *Oh, my God, if I get caught in here, it's curtains for my career!* I thought, sweating bullets as I hunched down so they wouldn't glimpse my head over the top of the stall. *Not going to do my marriage any good either. Imagine the headline on the front page of the* St. Louis Post-Dispatch: Pervert Ad Exec Caught In Anheuser Busch's Ladies' Room.

Standing stock-still on the toilet I said as many prayers as I could remember while having visions of cops cuffing and manhandling me into the back of a squad car. Though it couldn't have been more than a couple of minutes, it seemed like the women took hours in there, all while my career was flashing before my eyes. Finally I heard the sound of their voices tapering off and the door shushing shut behind them.

I quietly dismounted, left the stall, crept to the door, and stuck my head out. Coast was clear. But I still had to make it out of the ladies' room without anyone noticing. Scurrying out, I let the door close behind me and then ever so casually sauntered down the hall as though nothing untoward had happened.

Despite the harrowing experience, I managed to blow the presentation out of the water, making a terrific first impression on the chairman and giving my career a leg up. And to think what could have happened on that Wednesday in St. Louis.

If I can live through that, I can get through anything, I decide.

After a week of dealing with John's verdict, I'm finally at a place where I think I've settled the experience into a sensible perspective. Which is good since I run into Grisham at a party not long after, and he asks, "You okay? I slammed you pretty hard."

"Did sting a bit," I admit, mastering the art of understatement.

"Yeah, I've been there. It's no fun. You know I asked Renée whether I was being too rough, and she said that friends should be totally honest."

"You certainly were that," I say, coming up with a smile. "I appreciate it, thanks."

"Let's get a drink," John says, steering me to the bar, and that's the last we talk about it.

CHAPTER 8

Moving On

In Virginia, August is a scorcher, and people flock to the beach for relief. You can break a sweat raising your arm. AC blasts everywhere, and energy use is off the charts. Garden parties, which some misguided people insist on throwing, are hilarious because even though everyone comes dressed to the nines, pretty soon the men's shirts are black with sweat, and the women's hairdos are sagging and their makeup's running. Before long, jackets come off, ties are pulled down, blouses are unbuttoned, and everyone consumes more alcohol than they should, all the while making stupid jokes about "hydrating" as they order up more drinks from the bar.

I have to run up and turn on the air conditioner in my studio first thing in the morning, even before I make coffee; otherwise, the sweat dripping off my nose will short out my keyboard. Don't laugh. It's happened more than once.

August weather once compelled me to swear I would never return to the accursed Commonwealth of Virginia. I was a college kid attending officers' training at Quantico, a flat and desolate no-man's land of asphalt punctuated by barracks and surrounded by swamps. The drill instructor would wake us up before dawn, screaming such niceties as, "Drop your cocks and grab your socks!" We'd quickly dress in full gear and scramble out into formation in the dark outside the barracks with the DI yelling salacious remarks about our mothers and gender.

Before the sun lifted over the swamp, the first couple of laps around the parade ground were a breeze, actually kind of enjoyable if you like manly chants that rhyme different parts of the female anatomy while you double time in the dark carrying a full pack, a canteen, an ammo belt, and an M-1 rifle with a seven-pound steel hat on your head.

But the minute the sun rose, the parade ground turned into a blast furnace, and a million mosquitoes swarmed out of the swamp. To the bugs, we were sitting ducks since we couldn't swat them. If you tried, you'd be down on the asphalt doing a hundred pushups with the DI cursing at you and the rest of the platoon double-timing in circles around you, shooting daggers at you with their eyes.

So much for resolve. Here I am not only back in the Commonwealth in the month of August but also up in my studio trying to get started on another draft of *Sleeping Dogs*. I'm going into the second year of writing a novel that was supposed to take me five months, while in the recesses of my brain I'm wondering whether I should have opted for croquet or winemaking.

But there's no turning back now that John's invested hours in my manuscript. At least I owe it to him to turn it around. Not to mention myself.

I tear it apart and sort it into separate piles. Into the landfill go the pages on Knowles, the sections repeating Collyer's antics at the Pentagon, the goons in the black Suburbans, and the motel scenes featuring the nonstop drooling that John so much appreciated. I group the chapters on the intelligence agencies, programming them for rewrites to strip out my personal anti-government bias and give the characters dimension. When I finish, seven piles are neatly arrayed on my studio floor. Staring at them for a good hour, I'm perplexed at where to begin and feeling increasingly uncertain of whether I can pull it off, even with another year.

What happened to the vision of novel writing as a glorious act of creation with rays of light streaming down from on high and a string section playing in accompaniment? It's been replaced by the mundane piecework of tedious and time-consuming revision.

I'm sure at one time or another every writer's found himself in the consternating situation of staring at a screen or a sheet of paper and discovering his imagination's on empty. There's nothing more frustrating than writer's block. The computer seems to be laughing at you, mocking your misery as you tentatively reach for the keyboard again and again but, finding your mind a total blank, retract your hands in defeat. No matter how hard you try to jumpstart your brain, it won't even turn over.

I decide I'm suffering from a rare form of writer's block called "reviser's block," as I face down seven stacks of paper that keep taunting me, daring me to pick up one of them and begin. But I can't find the inner inspiration. Instead, all I hear is a creepy voice that keeps repeating, *Maybe you're not up to this, Tony. If it's too hard for you, give up. Don't even try.*

Another half hour goes by. I gaze out at the Southwest Mountains. The sky is a washed-out blue, the color it gets when it's 98 in the shade. Usually the mountains are inspiration. Today, I they're giving me a big goose egg. *This is getting ridiculous.*

Then I have an idea. *Men's group.*

I decide to take John's critique to the six of us who've been meeting for more than a decade, twice a month, on Tuesday nights from 6 to 7:30. After so many years we've become the closest of friends, and we share everything about our lives, insulated by an ironclad confidentiality agreement. What happens in men's group stays in men's group, so we're free to let everything hang out.

Anne was initially hesitant about my joining. She was concerned that I'd divulge intimate details about our relationship. But over time she came to appreciate how positive the experience was and decided that any intrusions on her privacy could be overlooked.

It's a great collection of characters, all within ten years of each other, all over the hill. There are two shrinks, Bob and Joe. Bob's a former UVa scatback, the scourge of the gridiron.

Joe's a big guy, a former basketball star. Bruce owns a successful local construction company. Dan was a publisher who
founded *Albemarle Magazine* and is a now a stockbroker.
Tom's a former commodity trader from Chicago. And then
there's me, the recovering ad guy. We're all reasonably happy
and well adjusted. The majority are married except for Dan,
who's divorced, and all are heading into the scary transition
from middle age to the uncharted waters beyond.

People ask me if we drink at the sessions, unable to imagine six guys getting together without a couple of six packs.
But the beverages go as far as coffee or tea with an occa-
sional Coke thrown in. We sit around Bob's office sharing
experiences about our relationships with our wives or our
children, or about work—whatever's eating at us. We start
with each member talking for ten or twenty minutes about
what's going on in his life. Sometimes there's a kid who has
OD'ed on booze or drugs or gotten into a scrape with the
law, has relationship problems, or is failing in school. We
talk his dad down and help him develop more perspective
on the situation so he can deal with it effectively.

Occasionally there are marital problems, and that's
where the group dynamic really comes into play. Women
easily share their feelings; men are loath to. So while wives
can find solace and understanding with their friends,
husbands keep their feelings to themselves, bottled up,
so they can too easily boil over. Our group is a sounding
board, a way to gain a more objective read on what's really
happening in a relationship and develop tactics to resolve
the problems.

Sometimes everyone's doing fine, so we sit around and chew the fat about politics, sports, or the economy. Or I bring in copies of John's critique of my first draft and pass them out.

I wait until they've had a chance to skim through the five pages, then say, "I'm in a better place with John's comments than I was a week ago. I can tell you that. But I sit in my studio and stare at the damn pages for hours. I just can't seem to get the motor going."

You can take their reactions right to the bank because no one has an agenda, no ax to grind—you're getting it straight.

Joe's first. He never pulls any punches. "Maybe you're scared shitless, ever thought of that?"

"You think?"

"Hell, I would be. Someone like Grisham takes you to the woodshed and you have to go back and do it again?"

"I'm with Joe," Bob says. "Just allow yourself to be scared, don't fight it. It'll get better."

Dan's a writer, so I'm looking forward to his reaction. "You know, when you look at his comments, it's not that bad. Most have to do with housekeeping. Simple stuff. Repetitions, fact checking, crap like that. Now he does nail you on sermonizing and plot construction, but that's fixable. Everything's fixable. Grisham says it himself."

Bob chimes in, "It's sort of like being down thirty-six points in the third quarter, and the coach tells you that you have to execute better. There's truth to that. It's no fun. But you can pull it out, Tony."

"Here's another perspective," Dan says. "I'd say you're damn fortunate to have someone who's as big a deal as John spend this much time on your project. You know what I mean? He could have taken one look at it and blown you off, told you he was too busy or something. He's put a lot of work into this, Tony. He obviously cares about you and your book."

I come back with, "It's just that he only liked 1 page out of 385."

"But isn't that what you were asking for?" Joe says. "Sugarcoating his comments wouldn't do you any good."

"I'm with Dan on this, Tony," Bob adds. "John's really being a true friend here. Someone who didn't care would tell you it's all great and go with it."

"Yeah, he didn't have to tell you a lot of it is crappy and needs work. He could have figured, 'I don't want to get involved in this,' and basically brushed you off, told you it's fine. Then you'd be worse off than you are now."

I never thought of it that way—I could be worse off than I am now. "This is helpful, guys, thanks."

"I mean, this is the shits getting dinged like this. I can tell it hurts," Tom says.

"Yup," I say, "but I guess I don't have any choice but to pick myself up and get to work."

"Look, the thing is, if writing novels was as easy as falling off a log, we'd all be set for life like John Grisham," Bob says, flicking the pages with his hand. "Fact is, it's damn tough. After reading this, it's harder than I ever imagined. I'll tell you that."

"Well, guys, I really appreciate all your help," I say, realizing that I've undergone a sea change in attitude, going from feeling beaten up about John's comments to appreciating them. *They're right. I should feel lucky that John was so brutal. Someone who didn't care would have given me a pass. And as Dan says, a lot of it is simple housekeeping, not pick-and-shovel work but broom-and-dustpan stuff.*

And it's not like I haven't revised a few things before, I tell myself as I drive home, trying to pick myself up by the bootstraps, manufacture some moxie, make myself feel human again. I went through the reworking process hundreds of times in my ad career. It's thought of as a creative occupation, but in reality more than half of the business is revising. Hardly ever was work sold in the first meeting, so it was endless redoing. Fix this, change that, put more product in, reshape the ending so it flows, rewrite the dialogue so the housewife sounds friendlier. And you'd do it because the clients tell you to. They're paying the bills.

Only one time did I refuse a request. Found the strength to give a senior client the big N-O. Another potential career-ender, only this one didn't take place in a ladies' room.

Since Quaker was my biggest client, I spent a lot of time at Quaker Tower, an anonymous steel-and-glass building looming over the Chicago River. One day I had a command performance for a big Quaker muckety-muck who was too high up in the organization to bother with advertising. But since this was the Michael Jordan campaign for Gatorade, and they'd paid millions for him to be their pitchman, the executive vice president wanted a peek before it aired.

Everyone assured me this was simply a courtesy presentation, no dog-and-pony show necessary. So I took the elevator to the umpty-umpth floor where the top execs lived.

"Heard great things about this advertising. Looking forward to seeing it," the corporate kingpin said as I pushed the cassette into the video player. I ran the commercial once and then at his request, a second, third, and fourth time. The guy's face lit up like a little kid. It was infectious and fun to watch. A children's reggae choir sang, "We want to be like Mike," while Michael Jordan soared through the air sinking baskets.

"That's great. I love it. It's terrific," he enthused. I figured I was home free until he suddenly went serious. "Okay, only one comment. And it's non-negotiable." He paused dramatically. "We paid sixteen million dollars for the name 'Michael Jordan' so I want you to use his proper name, Michael. Change the jingle to: 'Be Like Michael.' Understood?"

"Be Like Michael." Are you effing kidding? I'd heard stupid comments from clients before. But this one took the cake. It was even more ludicrous than the question about the blank space on the storyboard.

Maybe, since he was laying out the sixteen mil, it was reasonable from his point of view, but it was absolutely preposterous from an advertising perspective. My agency would have become the laughing stock of the industry. *Be Like Michael?*

Had I been a peon at a large shop, I would have had to respond meekly with something like, "We'll look at that, sir," and retreat to powwow with my bosses, who would have either folded or gone back at the guy with more firepower. I wasn't sure whether the EVP was just exerting his authority or whether he was dug in. Either way, it was risky. Agencies have been fired for less.

But my name was on the door, so it was a gamble I had to take. "Sorry, I can't do that."

"What?" the exec blurted, astonished that someone would refuse his direction.

"I can't change it to 'Be Like Michael.'"

"Why not?" he stammered.

"Because 'Be Like Michael' doesn't rhyme."

The Quaker exec whirled around to glare at me and disdainfully muttered, "You damn creative guys are all the same."

The brand team found a way for their boss to gracefully back off his demand, reassuring him that Michael Jordan's family and teammates all called him "Mike." The situation was resolved, the jingle stayed "Be Like Mike," and the commercials went on to sell the hell out of Gatorade.

Revising a novel is infinitely more complex than changing an ad, more like taking a car apart piece by piece, remachining engine parts, refitting the chassis, modifying the exhaust, and rejiggering the suspension—all in the hope that when you finally reassemble it, the damn thing will start and run smoothly. Just like I have no way of knowing whether, after I submit my second draft, Grisham will send me back to the showers or bless it and tell me to FedEx it to Gernert.

When I return from men's group, Anne's on the porch having a glass of wine. "How's my favorite zombie?" she says as I join her, making it clear I haven't done too good a job of hiding my feelings over the past week. "Wait," she says, sitting up in her chair to check me out. "Where's the hangdog look? You almost look normal."

"The guys were a big help."

"Good, I'm glad someone was. So you're going to give up the 'woe is me' business and go back to being good old Tony again?"

"Yeah, I think it's about time."

"I'd say. I tell you, another week like that and I would have been out of here."

"I hear you."

"You have to ask yourself if you want to keep this writing business up if it brings you down like this. It's not worth it. Go do PEC full time or something, but life's too short to put yourself through that kind of misery."

"I'm back on track now. I'll be fine."

"I hope so, because you know what?"

"What's that?"

"I love you."

"I love you, too."

"Good, so go get yourself a glass of wine and come join me. It's a lovely night."

CHAPTER 9

Climbing Out

I start with the seven stacks on my studio floor. The landfill pages get a healthy dose of the delete key. Highlight, strike. Highlight, strike. It actually feels liberating and vaguely curative, like taking a colonic cleanser at a tony spa. I watch days of writing vaporize with each keystroke.

Of course there's the reality that they have to be replaced. I can't have a 215-page book. And I can't sermonize for pages or get up on my soapbox, nor can I milk the intelligence wars—John's made that abundantly clear. I have to write tighter than ever but still stretch the novel out to close to 400 pages.

John said he's had lots of plots that ran out of energy before attaining the necessary length. "Some damn fine stories but they did not make it. Came up short," he's said a couple times, his voice sounding wistful, almost as if they were children who'd died early deaths.

Some years later, when I read his collection of novellas titled *Ford County*, I realized these were examples of the plots he was referring to. They were great stories with terrific characters and offered, in my opinion, some of John's best writing, but they were lacking sufficient complexity or substance to be turned into full-blown novels.

Is Sleeping Dogs *going to run out of gas?* Then it occurs to me. *Back to the chapter outline, dummy. That's what it's there for.* I realized I hadn't really used the outline the way John instructed. I didn't continually update it by adding or subtracting chapters as the plot developed, which is why I had Risstup drooling in the motel room for hundreds of pages while everyone else knew his secret. That's how I got so far off base. I didn't do what John told me to.

I decide to start at the beginning with Howie and his legendary kick. John says I made too much of it. *What did he say exactly? Something like* "hard to believe one kick would make him a legend to generations of UVa fans, even though they've had little to remember over the decades." That's the one light note in his entire critique, and he's probably right. UVa had a true basketball star in Ralph Sampson; in football, well . . . Okay, so I'll back it down a bit, shade and undercut his prowess so his kick seems more remarkable. Watch this:

Every Virginia football fan alive at the time quickly forgot the field goals Howie missed that fall. As dependable and consistent as he was during his first three seasons, in his senior year he choked, twice failing to put the team over the top, and talk around campus was that Coach was considering auditioning a soccer standout as Howie's replacement. So the pressure was on as Howie loped out onto the field that day, snapping his chinstrap, listening to the roar of the crowd, praying that his right foot would come through for him.

Howie didn't disappoint. Instead, Howie went down in Virginia football history as the player who redeemed the season with his amazing kick and was memorialized with the nickname, The Boot, bestowed on him the next day by a sportswriter for the local rag, a handle which stuck to Howie throughout the almost four decades since his graduation. Howie never took his achievement too seriously for he knew that if the pigskin had tumbled one inch the other way, he would have been no more than another face in a yellowing team picture on the walls of Mem Gym. And he fully realized that his kick paled in comparison to the achievements of other Virginia football greats and would have been a minor footnote had it not been the only bright spot in an otherwise abysmal season.

Yes, I nailed that one. Now to get into some of the thornier stuff.

I put aside the fact that Grisham writes umpteen pages on a good day, and I spend a week honing the six pages in which I introduce Mehran, the foreign student who does endless workouts in the Rutgers swimming facility. The assistant swim coach notices him and suggests he try out for the varsity team. When Mehran rudely brushes him off, Coach Johanson figures he has a chip on his shoulder and gives up.

But he can't help watching the young man out of the corner of his eye. Opting for subtlety for a change, I foreshadow the al-Qaeda operative's intentions for the reader by having the swim coach draw the wrong conclusions.

It wasn't until one day when Johanson noticed him carrying a large bag of equipment that the exchange student's workout regimen finally made sense. As he watched Mehran sling the tank on his back, fit his buoyancy compensator and mask and slip into his flippers, all the exercises now added up—the wall squats were for lifting gear and climbing up boat ladders, the back flies so he could more easily shoulder a heavy tank of compressed air—yet one specific drill Mehran did while wearing his scuba gear baffled the coach.

At the diving pool he would take a twenty-pound barbell plate out of his bag, set it on the edge of the diving pool, jump in and get settled in the water before sliding the plate off and taking it down seventeen feet to the bottom. Over and over again, he would submerge it and swim it back up, gently depositing it on the edge of the pool as if it weighed no more than a nickel.

What could he possibly be training for? Unless it was recovering sunken treasure.

That's it! The kid obviously was in training for one of those treasure hunting expeditions. A company secures the rights to dive a wreck and recover the loot and wants to keep it secret until their mission is completed so competitors won't discover the location and raid it in the middle of the night. That's why the student was acting so strangely, Johanson decided. There must be big money involved, gold coins, bullion, gems— people have made millions.

That's what John's talking about when he says, *show, don't tell.* While the swim coach decides Mehran's a treasure hunter, the reader gets the idea something much more sinister is taking place. *Maybe having something to do with recovering a nuke lost under water?*

As I continue to revise, the ground under my feet starts to feel firmer. I take on the major challenge, gradually revealing more and more information about the bomb from Risstup so it all doesn't come in one clump.

The goons are gone, and the guys with the Uzis have been zapped with the delete button. Now it's just Sharon and her patient in the VA hospital. She befriends him, gets him chatting and sharing his past. Digging through the hospital files, she finds all the records on him are missing, with only the bare-bones facts remaining. She knows she has no choice but to mine the information out of the old guy bit by bit.

Two days ago, she talked the supervising nurse in the ward into backing down Risstup's dose, convincing her it wasn't good for his heart. That night, Sharon's gamble pays off.

Risstup suddenly fumbles for her hand, his fingers searching around in the bedclothes. Finding it, he grips tightly and turns his head to look up at her, a look of near panic in his eyes. She watches as the eighty-some-year-old man's lips part and he says, slowly and haltingly, his head straining up off the pillow, "You have to help me."

"Yes, Major."

"Bomb . . ."

"Come again?"

"The bomb. You have to help me find the bomb."

Sharon looks at him quizzically, "A bomb? What bomb, Major?" What she's hearing makes no sense, but Risstup seems so disconcerted she has to take him seriously.

"If someone else found it, they could use it against us."

"I don't understand. Where is this bomb and who would use it against us?"

"It's lost. I lost it from my plane."

"When? How did you lose it?"

He shakes his head, frowns, then grimaces. He looks pained, his features contorting as if he is desperately trying to dredge up the information but is only getting a busy signal. His hand slipping out of hers, his head sinks back on the pillow.

Risstup has cracked the door open for Sharon. At her apartment after work, she Googles "lost bombs" and finds Howie's website, sleepingdogs.us.

In forty-five minutes, after reading everything on the site and checking through its links, she knows more than she needs to about lost nukes. Opening the fridge, she decides it's sandwich night and gets out the fixings, in the meantime tracking back over what she's learned. Eleven nuclear weapons lost during the ten years from '58 to '68. Dropped from British Columbia to North Carolina. Sharon does the arithmetic on Risstup's age. He would have been in his thirties.

"Damn," she says out loud, pausing with the knife halfway into the mayonnaise jar. "He could have been piloting one of those planes."

Then good sense prevails. *I'm imagining things. It's totally farfetched*, she thinks, far too level-headed to give credibility to conspiracy theories, but Collyer's website and the links to other sites about lost bombs certainly point in that direction. *I'm normally so sensible, what's going on with me?* Then she thinks of the major lying helplessly in Ward 3 and decides *I can't let anything happen to him, I'd feel guilty for the rest of my life.*

Eudora Welty once said, "You're not writing unless you surprise yourself." And that's what I'm doing, stripping away all the writing static, all the noise I usually put on the page, and simply telling the story by having the characters interact with each other, truthfully and in an uncomplicated manner so they come alive on the page. *Am I starting to get the hang of this writing thing? Damn, I think I am.*

It's late September and football season is in full swing. John and Renée have a box at the UVa stadium, which saves the day since the team too often puts on a disappointing show, and beers, brats, and good friends make up for botched plays and missed passes. It's a fun five hours, a chance to hobnob with the governor or athletic director, football stars from yesteryear, and sometimes a senator or two who wander into the suite.

Neither John nor I bring up *Sleeping Dogs.* What is there to say? John told me to take a year rewriting. I've got my work cut out for me.

A month and a half into my second draft, I suddenly trip and fall flat. I've revised the scene in which Howie and Sharon kidnap Risstup from the VA hospital so the writing's crisp and tense. Now I'm describing the Pentagon, and I find myself making up stuff Grisham or any astute reader would see through in a second. I've read everything I can get my hands on about the five-sided structure, but I'm having no luck bringing its corridors and offices to life. Fortunately, I happen to have a tenant who's an Army lawyer assigned to the JAG law school in town.

"Tim, it's Tony," I say to him on the phone. He and his family live in one of our houses and keep their horses in our paddocks and barn. He told me once he goes to meetings in what's often called the "Squirrel Cage" since that's what it looks like from the air. We catch up on news, and then I ask, "I need to take a peek inside The Building for this book I'm writing. Could I join you the next time?"

"What are you doing next Tuesday?" he asks. "If you're free, I can get you a visitor's pass."

The following week, while Tim goes about his business, I get a forty-five-minute tour from a PR officer that includes the entrance to the Secretary of Defense's office and the memorial to those who died in the 9/11 attack. I also get a look inside a couple of offices.

My lasting impression of the place is how damn shiny it is. Everything's polished to within an inch of its life.

Endless corridors with long stripes of ceiling fluorescents are reflected in the endless stretches of gleaming floors. There are more flags and colorful insignia than you can shake a stick at, and I've never seen so many hot and cold running generals all with multihued bunches of ribbons and medals on their chests. The public relations guy tells me it's called "fruit salad" in the military. Not surprising that the place looks cold and institutional, like a giant high school, but the couple of hours I spend there give me enough creative grist to begin to sketch in its character.

I use the impressions from the visit to begin revising the sections when the brass wakes up to the threatening situation unfolding at the VA hospital. To create a sense of the Pentagon and introduce the general who's riding herd on the lost nukes, I have a colonel walk a top-secret message to a secure area for transmission.

A slender and attractive secretary named Gretchen is standing at the water cooler reading *Vogue* magazine. The chief likes his secretaries trim and athletic and each day his staff starts with a 5:30 a.m. workout at the POAC, the Pentagon athletic club. She's an up and comer, slated for a position at the White House.

"Are you slumming, Colonel?" Gretchen asks the officer as he stops on his way to the secure area. "Don't see you often around here."

Wishnap holds up the envelope containing the document. "Got a Polo Step communication and I need a routing code."

"Polo Step, huh? How does it feel to be in the inner circle?"

"I'm afraid I'm just a messenger."

"You know what they say about messengers," she winks.

Their conversation is interrupted by a flurry of activity. The Chief of Staff, General Nerstand, is on the move, and it isn't healthy for the career of an aspiring army officer to be seen standing around the water cooler gossiping with one of the general's shapely young secretaries.

"See you, Gretchen," the colonel says, scurrying off in the direction of the file room before the flying wedge of brownnosers surrounding the senior officer in the United States Army sweeps through the area.

Opening the safe, he takes out the codebook and opens it. *Vector Eleven*, he wonders as his index finger pages down the sheet in the notebook and settles on the organization. *Wonder what in the hell Vector Eleven does?*

***

Kicking his feet up on the windowsill of his Pentagon office, the general stretches back in his chair. Out his office windows, Watt can see a fair number of cars in South Parking. Recently retrofitted with bombproof glass, the panes are now an inch thick and tinted a greenish yellow that bleaches out the color from the surrounding landscape so it looks like you're peering through dime store sunglasses. The lot is half full; at least he isn't the only one working on a Saturday.

Lieutenant General Greg Watt is not having a good day. For one thing he's sitting at his desk in the Pentagon instead of in the VIP box at Byrd Stadium watching the Terps play Clemson. In addition, the situation in Pittsburgh has gone from bad to worse. The nurse had become more suspicious. So the order went out to raise the dose and eliminate the problem.

It turned out to be too late.

Watt's heavily lidded eyes were the first to see the email to Vector Eleven from Pittsburgh. He shakes his head as he rereads it: At 2135 hours, a VA nurse, Sharon Thorsen, abducted Risstup from the hospital, escaping by drugging a member of the security detail. But why? Out of sheer goodness? Or does she have another agenda—maybe one backed by CIA or another agency hoping to dig up some dirt on the Defense Department?

Watt checks his watch. Almost 1600 hours. In a few minutes, the video from the security cameras will be electronically transmitted.

John took me to task for having Howie hang out in one place too long—Starbucks, the motel—so I have him move Sharon and Risstup in the middle of the night from one fleabag to another. I have warning stickies plastered all over the face of my computer that read "Show, Don't Tell," "Slow Down," "Read Dialog Out Loud Until It Sounds Real," and "Stop Preaching!" I'm determined to make the manuscript sing this time, and so I write:

Off Ross Avenue, the Pine Log Motel looks perfect. In the early morning light, Howie can tell it's not only inconspicuous down a narrow side street, but also nicely dilapidated, with its paint peeling and windows dingy and "vacancy" signboard dangling by one hook.

He wakes up the owner by holding his finger on the bell as the clumsily handwritten card tacked over it directs: "Keep on buzzing 'til I show, I'm here and I want your business." The owner comes to the door rubbing his eyes, his torso bare and pajama bottoms loosely knotted around his hips. He's probably forty but years of hard living make him look sixty. Before the owner even opens his mouth, Howie can tell he's found his next hideout.

"I'd like three rooms," he says.

The owner has to scratch himself in a couple of places before he can respond. "That'll be forty-four-fifty a night per room plus county lodging tax."

"Three rooms. I'll pay upfront for two nights."

The owner gives him a once over. "You ain't into drugs, are you?" he asks, wobbling around behind the pine paneled counter, hitching up his pants as he heads for his reservation book. "Don't take no offense, but there are too damn many meth dealers around these days. Blow themselves to kingdom come and burn a place to the ground before you know it."

"We're just tourists. Traveling through with my dad and daughter. Hope to do a little hiking." He gets a grunt of satisfaction in return.

Checking the calendar on my studio wall, I realize it's been six months since I started on the new draft. I'm making progress on the revision with my hands firmly on the wheel. John made it clear that Osama needed to be revealed gradually. I stow my sledgehammer and wait until I'm three-fifths into the book to include him.

I have Mehran, the swimmer and Rutgers student, secretly meet with Jamal, a senior al-Qaeda operative, in a warehouse in New Brunswick. I'm not only setting up the final scene of the novel when Mehran goes after the bomb, but I'm foreshadowing his action and linking up with the information I gave the reader in the swim coach's observations at the Rutgers pool.

Jamal leads Mehran around the shop proudly displaying his machines and explaining their functions. He stops at a row of three long, dull-green, metal tubes lying in steel and wood gantries. Mehran recognizes them immediately.

"Of course you are familiar with these weapons. These are obviously mockups but the dimensions are precise right down to the millimeter."

"Yes," Mehran says, putting his hand on the cone of the first bomb in the row, eager to display his knowledge. "This is the Mk-28, a hydrogen bomb yielding 70 kilotons to 1.1 megatons of explosive force. And this is the Mk-39," Mehran says, pointing at the next. "Produced in two configurations, three megatons and four. The third is an Mk-15 mod 0, the first lightweight hydrogen bomb, twelve feet long and just under four tons."

"You have done your homework. I have replicated these since they were the models carried in SAC bombers during the years in question. So we will be prepared for any eventuality. When we ascertain the model of the bomb you will be dealing with, I will furnish you with my outstanding achievement." Jamal nods proudly as he reaches up and takes down a spun aluminum ring—in the shape of a life preserver but much larger in diameter—from an overhead rack where a long row of similar rings hangs.

"Here it is," he says, cradling the object in his hands. Satiny and lustrous, its exterior is rounded while its inner surface is perfectly flat. Carefully sliding the ring down over the cone of the Mk-15 until it clicks into place against the steel skin of the bomb, he explains, "The same way the Americans used a shaped charge of TNT to activate the atomic primary stage, I have designed a collar to the dimensions of each bomb."

Looking around the workshop as if someone might be watching, he leans in and whispers in Mehran's ear, switching from English to Arabic.

As he listens, Mehran is dazzled with Jamal's brilliant breakthrough. In a million years the Americans could never imagine what Jamal has conceived for them. They think their sleeping dogs can't be awakened. But with Jamal's collar, Mehran will prove them wrong.

I'm energized by how everything's coming together. The reader knows that Mehran has been practicing bringing a barbell plate up from a pool bottom. Now they can put two and two together and figure out Mehran is planning to swim the collar to the bomb, and that the collar will provide the detonative force to compensate for the degradation of the TNT. The collar's a little Tom Clancy military/technology riff that adds veracity to the story. And al-Qaeda is waiting for Collyer to lead them to it so they can put Mehran to work.

At the new motel, Howie and Sharon quiz Major Risstup and gradually help him to reveal details about piloting a B-52 in order to enable the pilot to clear his fogged memory so that he can reveal where he dropped the bomb. Howie's worked up a simulation of a B-52 cockpit on his computer to set the scene for Risstup. Finally catching on to John's "show, don't tell" axiom, I impart the info about the B-52 by staging a scene with Collyer and the pilot doing a simulated takeoff. Though there's no actual bomber, I'm able to give the reader a feeling of what it's like to get one of those monsters off the ground and up into the air. "Showing" and not "telling" is finally coming alive for me.

Howie swivels the laptop toward him. "Let's try a takeoff and see what comes back to you."

"I'll give it a shot," Risstup says.

"Okay, Major Risstup, we're cleared for takeoff. Full throttle . . ."

"Full throttle," Risstup repeats, acknowledging the command.

Sharon stands behind the two as the plane speeds down the runway, the landscape flashing by out the windows.

"With 48,000 gallons of fuel in the wings and a total weight of 488,000 pounds," Howie explains, "the B-52 chews up miles of runway in order to gain altitude."

"Actually," Risstup clarifies, "the wings get airborne first, and they sort of bully the huge wheel trucks up off the ground."

"We're airborne," Howie says. "Landing gear up, Major."

"Landing gear up," Risstup repeats.

"Give me the course, Major."

No response from Risstup.

"The course, Major Risstup," Howie prompts him again.

Risstup scowls.

"You were doing fine, Mark. You were right there with me."

Risstup throws up his hands. "I know, but I lost it. I'm sorry. I want to help, but after a while everything goes blank."

"Maybe we can try again later," Sharon suggests.

Having played lacrosse for five years in school and college, I look forward to February because not only does it mean the end of winter, but the start of lax season. While the game's radically changed, the weather hasn't. Whether playing or watching, you go from shivering in February to sweating in May. Our equipment used to be leather helmets, football cleats, and sticks that were heavy oak clubs, their rawhide and gut pockets crafted by Canadian Indians. Now the players wear plastic helmets, featherlight shoes, and carry high-tech sticks made from exotic alloys with nylon and plastic pockets. And the size of lacrosse players has skyrocketed. The majority are more than six feet tall. While academically I imagine I might be able to squeak back into Yale, I'd never play lacrosse, as I'd be a midget among giants. UVa has a perennially strong program, having won the NCAA championship a bunch of times, so it's some of the best lacrosse in the country and a helluva lot of fun to watch.

While the new season sprouts around us, I'm racing to the finish line with *Sleeping Dogs*, knitting the various subplots together, heading toward the three-hundred-page mark, when one bright spring morning I get a call. It's the president of the Piedmont Environmental Council, Chris Miller. He came on board in the mid '90s to spearhead the Disney fight and has continued to work miracles for us. A unique combination of talents, he's smart as a whip, a policy guru, an engrossing presenter, a consummate fundraiser, and a skilled grassroots organizer.

"You sitting down?" he asks.

"That good, huh?"

"As bad as you can imagine."

The PEC's crown jewel is more than 300,000 acres of private property up and down the Piedmont that we've protected with conservation easements. Instead of strip malls and subdivisions littering the countryside, our nine-county area has some of the most pristine landscape in the country.

"The Energy Department has just announced a new national transmission policy," Chris continues.

"What now?" I ask. The Bush Administration has been blaming states for dragging their feet on power line proposals, tagging them with the responsibility for blackouts. For a while we've suspected they had some noxious new strategy up their sleeve.

"They've opened up basically the entire area, not just Virginia but also New York, Pennsylvania, and Maryland, to new lines, and not just a strip of land either. I'm talking about whole states."

Since Virginia is situated between a bunch of power plants in the Ohio Valley and the huge energy-consuming populations of the Eastern Seaboard, new demand from New York, New Jersey, and New England could generate proposals to string new transmission lines across northern Virginia, right over the farms, parks, and forests we've worked so hard to protect for the past thirty years.

"How exactly?" I want to know.

"By using the federal power of eminent domain. Say a state like Virginia doesn't okay a power line within a year, the feds can come in and seize the land to clear the way for the utility."

"Is that legal? Isn't that tromping all over states' rights?"

"We think so, but we'd have to go to court to prove it."

I try to look on the positive side. "It's going to be easy to get people up in arms over this one. First line that's proposed we can get people raising hell."

"Unfortunately, that's the worst part. We can rile people up 'til the cows come home but these guys are not elected. They don't have any oversight. There's no way to get to them."

"So what options do we have?" I ask.

"That's why I'm calling," Chris says. "We can sue the Energy Department, raise a ruckus in the legislature, and make our case before the State Corporation Commission, but as you know, nine times out of ten the SCC does the utilities' bidding. What I'm telling you is we don't have much traction here."

In all the other challenges we've undertaken, we've been able to build a groundswell of support from concerned citizens. We've never gone into a fight without grassroots involvement.

"You're saying it's a lost cause?"

"No, just that it will be a long, tough, expensive fight with no guarantees we'll come out on top, so we'd better make damn sure we're up to it."

"Where does Eve come out?" Eve's the PEC chair, a gray-haired, grandmother type who's tough as nails, a great horsewoman and foxhunter who, though she couldn't possibly tip the scales at more than a hundred pounds soaking wet, can still throw her weight around and make things happen.

"She's left it up to me. She's okay either way," Chris says. "That's why I'm calling you. I need some pushback."

"Look," I tell Chris, "from my point of view we're screwed either way. We can't lie down and let them roll over us because people depend on us to stand up and fight. If we don't, they'll say we've gone chicken and that will be the end of us, curtains, bye-bye PEC. And if we raise a bunch of money and go against them, but they build the line anyway, we're toast too."

"But we have to level with people that it's going to be expensive and uphill all the way."

"How much?" I ask.

"A million . . . two million . . . three. We'll cost it out. The lawsuit alone could cost a million."

"That's real money," I say, knowing how challenging fundraising's going to be. I imagine asking our supporters, *Hey, how about giving us five grand to fight a power line that will in all likelihood be built anyway?*

I'm finding myself wishing Chris hadn't pulled me into this mess. Starting to see glimpses of the finish line with my book, I'm counting on getting the second draft to John by summer's end. Having to get involved in a major PEC battle is going to cut into my writing time.

The decision is made for us a couple of weeks later when the folks from Dominion Power pay a visit to our main office in Warrenton. They have the gall to request we step aside while they erect their 175-foot-high towers to march across our splendid vistas of conserved land. And they add insult to injury by insinuating that if we don't, we'll be responsible for rolling brownouts and likely blackouts that will put Virginia's economy in the crapper.

What they don't know is that we've assembled a crack team of energy experts who suspect the power company has cooked the books to come up with numbers justifying the brownout threat. Plus, ominous signs point to an economic slowdown, which means there will be a tapering off in energy demand rather than an increase. There's no reason for another four-billion-dollar power line subsidized by the ratepayers if the economy's going down the tubes.

So instead of sidelining us, Dominion's waved a red flag in front of our noses and made us hopping mad. The board unanimously votes to go to war.

Fortunately I've done all my research so I can write all morning and devote my afternoons to the power line fight. I'm on the last chapter, cranking up the tension with all three adversaries on the lookout for the bomb. From quizzing Major Risstup, Howie figures out the location and now is out on the Chesapeake Bay. He's ostensibly looking for the bomb, but in actuality he's acting as a decoy hoping he'll draw out al-Qaeda. The good guys are putting two and two together and are gradually learning what al-Qaeda's up to. Straub and Jimmick, the DHS head, give the reader the latest update.

"Al-Qaeda found someone familiar with the bomb and had him design some device the suicide diver could attach to it."

"Something filled with C-4."

"Yeah, at a point where the bomb is most vulnerable."

"We have to find out exactly what they were making in that warehouse."

"The FBI is flying a mechanical engineering guru in from Carnegie Mellon."

"Couldn't we have found someone locally? Howie's out there now," Straub says, looking up at the monitor. The fog's burning off, and as he zooms in he can see the boat chugging out of the harbor into Herring Bay.

"We struck out with two local guys. Scratched their heads for a couple hours but couldn't put it together."

Now is the perfect time to reveal bin Laden's involvement. Almost at the end of the novel, bringing him in not only adds another layer of suspense and intrigue but also forces the president's involvement. Jimmick and Straub continue to move the plot forward:

"Where is the Saudi now?"

"Flew yesterday afternoon to London from Philly on his way back to Saudi Arabia."

"The FBI must have just missed him."

"It was close. His flight landed in Jeddah four hours ago."

"Jeddah—shit."

"What about it? This Jamal guy grew up there."

"I was afraid you'd say that." Now Straub knows he has no choice but to hedge his bets. "I think we need to clue the boss in. Tell him it's time to play Paul Revere."

"You're changing the plan."

"You're damn right."

"Why?"

"Jeddah's where bin Laden's from," Straub says as he quickly zooms back out so Howie's boat is a speck on the bay, wondering how the president of the United States will react to the news that there is a fully armed four-megaton hydrogen bomb mere miles from the White House and chances are Osama bin Laden knows more about it than he does.

Going for a socko ending, I've put the swimmer in the water heading for the bomb with a Coast Guard Jayhawk chopper hovering over him. The reader knows he's holding the explosive collar, that he can swim like a fish, and hold his breath for hours. Will he make it to the bomb or will the helicopter's machine guns blow him out of the water?

Twenty feet below the surface, Mehran silently glides toward his rendezvous point, the collar tucked in tight to his body, his powerful legs gracefully sweeping the monofin up and down as they race him through the water. He quickly checks the GPS readout on his wrist receiver. Less than forty yards remaining. His body is behaving beautifully, just as it was trained, his lungs not yet screaming for air, his mind clear and focused on the prize ahead. He ducks his head so the water at the bottom of his mask sloshes up and clears the glass. Though the water is murky, through the gloomy haze faint outlines of an object ahead come into focus. Long and cylindrical, it sits askew in the sand, as if it had settled in at an angle. He struggles to keep his heart rate under control.

"Lieutenant Waite, do you see him? Do you see anything?" Jimmick shouts into his handset.

"No, sir. Nothing yet," Waite reports as he circles a hundred feet off the surface, the two other helos on his port and starboard. "How long can this character stay under water? It's been seven minutes already. He can't last much longer."

Neither can I, Straub thinks, checking his wristwatch again.

I end the novel with an unexpected twist: While the terrorists are foiled, the intelligence agencies continue to cover up the existence of the bomb. But Howie locates it and confronts the president. He's a hero and goes down in history for forcing the administration to clean up the lost nukes.

I go over and over the manuscript then print it out and hand it to Anne. I know John's facing revisions of his newest legal thriller, so I'm eager to get it to him before I lose him for a month.

"I'll read it if you want, but I'm sure it's fine, Tony," Anne says. "Time to get John's take on it."

She's right, of course. Aren't wives always right? And this time, I don't have to agonize about Grisham's reaction. After all, I've spent a year on the rewrite, four or five hours a day, Monday through Friday, a rough calculation results in more than 1200 hours of sitting at the keyboard slaving away on the novel. After being soundly beaten about the head and shoulders with his last critique, I've worked the manuscript over exhaustively. I've crossed every "t" and dotted every "i." I'll be astonished if John can find one damn typo or goof-up.

So I drop off the box at Oakwood Books feeling supremely confident that I have a bestseller on my hands. It's going to Gernert, he'll do an auction, publishers will be falling all over themselves to land the book, the advance money will start rolling in, and you'll soon see my mug across from Matt Lauer's on TV.

While I'm jazzed about the novel, the power-line fight is hitting speed bumps. PEC is being ghettoized by much of the environmental community. Even the pols who are our friends are wagging their fingers at us.

One state senator with whom I'm on a first-name basis calls me and says, "Tony, I can't help you on this one. I think you'd better fold your tent."

"I'm telling you, the utility's numbers don't hold up."

"Look, if we don't build that line and there's a blackout, I wouldn't be able to get elected dogcatcher. I'm all for the environment, but the current's running too strong on this one. I'm sorry, but that's just the way it is."

Everyone's drinking the utility's Kool-Aid. But our experts tell us the numbers don't justify a new line. Fortunately our board stands firm, particularly those members who are threatened with 200-foot towers on their farms. We decide to go ahead.

Our lobbyist's office in Richmond becomes the war room. The scene is right out of one of John's novels. Piles of documents stacked everywhere, coffee cups and empty soda cans all over the place, even a cot in one corner for catnaps. It's David and Goliath time with our team of four up against the hundreds of highly paid lawyers and energy experts from Dominion and outside firms. And they play hardball by encouraging counties not affected by the proposed line to support it, with the clear implication that they could always change the location—maybe run it through your county? They run expensive ads threatening brownouts and sic their PR firms on politicians in Richmond.

Their flacks trumpet that America has an antiquated energy delivery system that's hampering our economic well-being, and only with investments in new transmission can we keep up with developing nations like China and India.

It's tough sledding for the PEC because no matter how staunch an environmentalist you might be, no one enjoys power outages, which often mean lugging buckets of water to flush toilets and emptying rotten food out of freezers. So as ugly as power lines and transmission towers may be, people accept them as the visual costs of our creature comforts.

We need to find a hook to engage grassroots opposition, something that will shock people out of seeing the power line as a necessary evil.

And in the meantime, I wait for the phone to ring. By now, John's had the book for three weeks.

CHAPTER 10

Still No Cigar

I don't waste any time getting down to his office when he calls. As John hands me the cardboard box containing my manuscript, I ask, "So what do you think?"

"Vastly improved," is all he says, with an absolutely straight face, not a trace of emotion, and before I can quiz him, his assistant interrupts with a question, and they excuse themselves and hustle off to take care of something, leaving me standing in the lobby with my thumb up my novel.

While "vastly improved" sure beats "piece of crap," it reeks of faint praise I decide as I head toward the parking lot. He didn't say, "It's terrific," or "You knocked it out of the park." Instead he put it at the higher levels of "improved," which can only mean I have more work to do—the last thing I want to hear.

Sitting in the car, I open the box and take out the envelope lying on top of the manuscript. It has Grisham's name and address in the upper left corner and "Tony" scrawled in the middle.

I open the envelope, unfold the pages and begin to read.

John Grisham   28 August 06

Tony:

    This draft is much better. The story is tighter, more focused, leaner and moves quicker. But there are still some areas of concern. I've left most of my notes on the manuscript, but I'll cover the big thoughts below:

    1.   Balance: It still feels like 2 major stories - Howie and the nukes, and the intel games in Washington. I didn't count pages, but it seems as if the cloak and dagger stuff in DC gets more play. While this should certainly be the major subplot, it cannot rival Howie/Risstup.

    2.   Pacing: Although the story takes 8 or 9 days, there are moments when you wonder what in the world they could possibly be doing in a motel room as the hours drag by. This needs to be condensed substantially. Risstup does nothing for the first 3 days. At one point, he seems to have said more in the hospital than he does in the motel room.

"Much better," is a hell of a lot preferable to "You should never submit a first draft." But I realize I still have a bunch of work to do on balance and pacing. I'm kind of chuckling to myself as I think back on when we began this adventure. Seemed like it would be so easy, and now almost two years later, I'm still pushing the rock up the hill.

    You will see a number of "detours" on the ms. David uses this word occasionally and I'd choke him I could get my hands on him. This is when the action stops, and virtually all detours are bad ideas. In your case, you have the habit of stopping the action and telling the reader about the characters involved in the action. There's way too much backfill. The reader will not care where some of your minor characters went to college or what they did in the military or anything about their wives.

    Repeat a thousand times, "Show, don't tell."

3. Length: I would seriously try to cut at least 50 pages. I didn't do the math, but my suggested cuts probably add up to 30 or 40.

Never be afraid to cut. I do it every time, and always for the better. Sure it was painful writing the stuff, but cutting can be rewarding too. You're making the book better.

4. Thorsen/Risstup: Thorsen's decision to join Howie, kidnap Risstup, and throw her career and life out the window is made over a cup of coffee. She needs to have much more invested.

"Detour," meaning action-stopping exposition, is a writing disease I hadn't heard of before. I'm interested to read the ms and see where he finds them. *Damn, and I thought I'd finally broken through the "show, don't tell" thing.*

Here's an idea: Strengthen the relationship between Thorsen and Risstup at the hospital. He tells her more about his past (this will save days in the motel rooms!) and she has such affection for the old guy that she doesn't hesitate to grab him when she's convinced he's going to be killed.

Here's another Grisham gem—he wants me to reinforce the relationship between Sharon, the nurse, and her patient, Major Risstup. When she gets close to him, she'll do anything to save him. Thank you for this suggestion, John.

5. Mehran: By page 47 we know exactly what he's up to. The suspense is gone. I would make him much more sympathetic in the beginning. Suspicious, yes, but also a cute kid with a cute girl who's enjoying life in America, plenty of sex and maybe even a beer now and then. Slowly add the suspicion.
Slowly show the reader what he's up to, don't scorch the reader with a nuclear blast on page 47.

6. Alphabet soup: Cut out some of the agencies. There are simply too many to keep up with. Sure they exist and they do all the stupid things you describe, but the reader can only absorb so much.

7. Roadblocks: These are worse than detours. On page 92 Mehran eases out of bed, eases to his study, closes the door behind him, sneaks to his computer, does some work, then, on page 93 glances over at Melanie to make sure she's asleep. Melanie, of course, is still asleep in the bedroom, which is somewhere beyond the closed door of his study.

These little mistakes stop the reader cold. And, worse, they make the writer look careless. Worse still, they make agents and editors curse.

The nature of editing is to point out the bad stuff, not to
mention the good. After 19 books, I still get furious with Renee
and David as I slave over a ms after they've had a delightful time
marking it up. It's just part of the process. A thick skin helps.

Here's another ailment I didn't know a manuscript could have—a "roadblock." But when he spells it out, I quickly leaf to pages 92 and 93 and dammit if he's not right. John's big blue scrawl reads, "Roadblock, the reader stops to figure this out." And here it comes again—that sheepish feeling of being caught making another stupid mistake.

But John picks me up in the next paragraph by saying the same thing my guys in the men's group did: editing is all about the bad stuff and you have to learn to take the lumps. His next comment takes me completely by surprise:

My advice is to do the next draft and start submitting. It
may not be a good idea to go back to David because he has already
passed on your earlier book. I'll be happy to discuss this with
him. I will also ask his advice on other agents, but only if you
wish.

I've enjoyed the project, but my input is over. I've read so
much about lost nukes that I found myself getting scenes confused
with earlier drafts and outlines. And, the editing can go on
forever, just as any sentence can be revised a hundred ways.

When you finish the next draft, let's have lunch and talk
about the submitting game.

I've been wishing that the endless process of revising would end, and now I've gotten my wish. But is he cutting me loose, putting distance between himself and my novel?

And what's this business with David Gernert? Does he know something I don't?

Since John's been absolutely frank and honest with me up to now, I decide there's no reason to doubt what he's saying. He's telling me I'm at the point where it makes sense to move to the next stage. And Gernert might not be the right agent after all is what he's saying. We'll just have to play that out.

In the meantime, it's slash-and-burn time for the manuscript with fifty pages destined for the dumper. Before I head home, I take a peek at the end of my pile of pages. Sure enough, there are notations in blue ink right up to the end. At least he read the entire book this time.

I'm going to attack the next draft first thing tomorrow. Right now I'm going to savor the sight of light at the end of the tunnel.

When I get into the manuscript, it's no wonder John's at the end of his rope with *Sleeping Dogs*. He's spent hours revising, and there are hundreds of notations throughout. But I'm encouraged that I don't see the first blue ink until page thirty-seven. Chapters one through four escape unscathed. When he does start to edit, he makes a couple of notes about the action dragging, then points out my first repeated word.

He nails me for overkill with Mehran and takes me to task for plot inconsistencies, catches places where there's too much exposition—*show, don't tell*—but all fixable and things I should have caught. Many of his comments are encouraging. He likes my description of the Pentagon and the fleabag motel, for instance, and makes positive comments about some of the action scenes.

Despite John's choice of the tepid phrase "vastly improved" to characterize the manuscript and his unsettling suggestion that Gernert might not be the right agent, I'm feeling buoyed up and confident. All I need to do is fix the problems and make the cuts, which will involve maybe a month's worth of work. And then we can have that lunch to discuss submission.

Submission—wow! I'm closing in on two years working on *Sleeping Dogs*. It was October of '04 that we had our kickoff lunch, and now it's a couple days into September '06.

As I head into the final lap, tidying up and making the cuts and corrections John has detailed for me, the two years seem like a worthwhile investment. I have a terrific idea, solid plot, good characters, and exciting action—all the elements of a successful thriller.

By the end of September, I've finished the manuscript and give John a ring.

"I'm swamped, under water with the revisions on my legal thriller, won't come up for air for at least three weeks," he tells me.

Fine, I'll spend the time going back through the manuscript with a fine-toothed comb, I think.

It's four weeks before we nail down a lunch date. Walking down the Mall together, he chooses a restaurant we've never been to, and he seems uncharacteristically edgy and preoccupied. I expected him to be chatty and cracking jokes the way he usually is, but he's acting like he'd rather be somewhere else. I expected all kinds of helpful suggestions on how I should market the book, but instead it's pulling teeth, and seems to be the last thing he wants to talk about.

At the end of the meal, over coffee, I finally lay it on the table. "About *Sleeping Dogs*—you said Gernert might not be the right agent for me. Talk to me about that. Because of all the agents I've submitted to, his agency has come the closest to buying my work."

"He passed on it. That's all. You might have a better shot with another agent."

"I hear you, but I feel like I should give him a try."

"Fine, if that's what you'd like, I'll tell David to take a look at it," John says. I'm feeling like there's something he's leaving out, but I'm not sure, so I drop it. *Is this the end of the line and John's washing his hands of my book?*

"I'll give you a ring after I talk with David," John tells me as we shake hands outside the restaurant. *Something's not right, but I'm not sure what it is. Maybe he's feeling under pressure from his revisions. Maybe his skin thinned out on him? Or does he not like the way my novel's turned out?*

"Look forward to hearing from you. Thanks."

Five days go by before he calls. "Send *Sleeping Dogs* up to David. I talked to him, and he'll be looking for it."

"Thanks, John, much appreciated."

"Oh, and another thing."

"You bet . . ."

"Keep your fingers crossed," John says. There's a tone to his voice that tells me, *You're going to need some luck on this one.*

"Of course," I say, "I'll do that." And we end the conversation.

Since David is reading my novel at John's request, I know I'll get a quick read. But who knows how many manuscripts he has in front of *Sleeping Dogs*? It's time for me to kick back and get a little Christmas shopping done. So I head into town.

Charlottesville's Downtown Mall is the former Main Street that the city planners closed to traffic to convert into a pedestrian walkway in the 1970s. It languished for a number of years until an out-of-town developer constructed, of all things, a hockey rink. Somehow the ice-skating proved to be a magnet, a movie theater and a steak joint followed, and in a couple years the once moribund Mall was thriving. Now it's a major attraction packed with people nearly around the clock.

Passing a rare coin shop halfway up, I get an idea. Hitchhiking on John's suggestion to keep my fingers crossed, I stop in and buy myself a good luck charm—a mint silver dollar. I'm putting the odds at 75-25 that David will take on my novel. After all, I have a direct line to him from John, but it can't hurt to have a little additional luck on my side.

It's no secret that the literary business is incredibly subjective. No one knows what dog-eared manuscript is going to morph into the next *DaVinci Code* or *Harry Potter* or which novelist typing away in some garret is going to burst on the scene as the new John Grisham or James Patterson. So agents and publishers have to bring their judgment, honed by years of experience, to bear on countless books. They cram bunches of pages into their briefcases to read on the train or at the beach and winnow through piles of manuscripts, ash-canning the majority of them while keeping an eye out for the next *Cold Mountain* or *The Firm*. It's a crapshoot for both the agents and the writers who submit to them, with high stakes and even higher odds.

Of course, the publishing gurus don't always get it right. There are the legendary stories of agents tricked by their own experience into snubbing future blockbusters. *Confederacy of Dunces* was one of the first rejected manuscripts to become a bestseller, and more recently Kathryn Stockett's *The Help* was turned down by more than sixty agents before someone finally came to her wits and realized its potential to sell mil-lions of copies. One agent supposedly told her, "People don't want to read about black help."

When I sent my manuscript for *Ads for God* out to a film studio exec friend in Hollywood, he read it and emailed me, "Stuff about advertising doesn't work. People don't want to read about it." Then along came *Mad Men*.

Subjectivity is a slippery slope. I once worked for a famous creative director who was reviewing a storyboard my group had done for a dog food commercial. The idea was two dogs walking around in heaven talking about how they preferred life back on earth except for one thing, the celestial taste of the kibbles we were peddling. The dialogue was great, and the storyboard captured the scene beautifully with two cute doggies strolling through the clouds. The art director had even added the delightful touch of small harps strapped to the canines' backs. While the creative director loved the board, his voice went gruff and he sneered at me, "Lose the harps, okay?"

Baffled by such a ridiculous request, I asked why.

"Because there are no harps in dog heaven," he said with not a hint of humor on his face—and this was from a guy who created "Like a good neighbor," "twoallbeefpatties," "You deserve a break today" and is in the Advertising Hall of Fame.

So anybody can get it wrong.

But despite the odds, I'm feeling I have the best chance I've ever had to get published. After all, I've had the most outstanding editor/mentor a writer could have, an entrée to a top agent, a solid idea, and a manuscript that's been manicured, primped, and polished to within an inch of its life.

One sunny day in December, I get the call. "Hi, Tony, it's David Gernert in New York." We exchange pleasantries, and then he gets down to business. "Look, I read your book. Do you want the good news first or the bad?"

Oh, shit. That's some choice.

"Let's go with the good," I reply. I have a stack of sticky notes and I'm scribbling like mad.

"It's the best thing you've written, a pretty damn good book. Has a good pace, really moves along. It's good enough to get published. I like it but . . ." and now David drops the bomb . . . "I don't love it."

When women tell you that they think you're a really nice guy, you get the point. And when agents say they don't love your book, you know it's the ball game. They have to think it's the best thing since sliced bread because publishers are deluged with material and quickly become jaded. Unless an agent can swear he has the next *Harry Potter*, they won't give him the time of day.

David goes on to explain, "There's a glut of thrillers out there . . ."

Strike one!

" . . . and terrorists are a tough row to hoe. Publishers are sick of them."

Strike two!

"And it's harder for me, because I represent John, and the expectations are high that I'm bringing them another Grisham, so it kind of works against a writer."

Strike three and I'm out! David's turning me down. My big chance has just evaporated in front of my eyes.

David continues, "But because *Sleeping Dogs* is a cut above everything we read here, I'd be happy to recommend it to other agents." This is the consolation prize. He knows I'm a friend of John's, so he's letting me down easy.

"That would be great. I'd appreciate it." *What else am I supposed to say?*

"I'll round up those names and email you in the next couple of days."

I thank David, say goodbye, and hang up, feeling like I've been socked in the nose. The one big chance I had, the hopes and dreams, the hard work, the emotional roller coaster rides, the psychic investment—all up in smoke.

And what's really eating me as I sort through my stickies is that David's comments are market driven and have nothing to do with my writing. Terrorists are out of vogue, the indus-try is saturated with thrillers, and editors are expecting the next Grisham from David so he can't submit anything less.

While I don't know this for sure, chances are that other agents will share David's point of view on terrorists and thrillers. If those are accepted myths in the business, *Sleeping Dogs* is a dead duck.

I suddenly realize the wisdom behind Grisham's invent-ing a new field of popular fiction—the legal thriller. Like it or not, stories with sleazy lawyers, corrupt judges, and jurors for sale never go out of style, and since he invented the category, he's the original. Others may glut the market but not John.

And this business about David recommending it to other agents—isn't that like handing someone a half-eaten plate of food and saying, "I didn't care for it, but you might."

While I'm "bitterly disappointed"—that's the cliché that comes to mind—I'm at the same time dreading the grim prospect of blind submissions to hordes of agents. Most won't look at manuscripts, so writers have to first submit a plot synopsis in what's called a query letter. If agents are interested, then they'll ask you to send the manuscript. So you have to send out a stack of queries and wait two to six weeks or longer for the form-letter responses inevitably tell-ing you to take a hike. And get this, you won't even hear back from them if you don't enclose what's termed in the trade a SASE, a self-addressed, stamped envelope. So it costs you to get shitcanned. Now you can get tossed in the dumper for free via email. But the time frame and pain are still the same.

Opening a rejection letter at the post office can wreck a good day, two can test your emotional stability, and three or more can make you want to go postal. I used to file them, but I decided that keeping rejection notices is like saving scabs. Now I toss them in the trashcan at the post office while I fake a hearty laugh like someone just told me a hilarious joke.

First I'm going to see what happens with David's agents. Weirder things have happened; maybe there's someone out there who will like his leftovers. Right on schedule he emails me. He's sent *Sleeping Dogs* to an agent who used to work at his shop and another whose name I immediately recognize. I'm keeping my hopes under a blasting mat to keep from being pulled down into the depths again. But I can't keep my mind from conjuring up all kinds of rosy scenarios. *This lady who used to work for Gernert, maybe since she has a new business, she'll look kindly on taking his castoffs? And this other agent, will he have a pal at a publishing house who just happens to be looking for a thriller about terrorists?*

Maybe there's an unpublished novelist out there who can keep his wits through this submission process and not spend hours conjuring up a million whacko scenarios. But I doubt it.

Within a couple of days, David forwards the critique from his former employee. It's the most thoughtful, well-composed, and respectful rejection notice I've ever received, full of reasoned reactions why *Sleeping Dogs* didn't work for her. She even thanked him for passing it on to her. It comes across as so mannerly, and seemingly painless, like dying in your sleep.

The second agent gets me chuckling, for he tries to interest me in his course on novel writing. Here I am trying to sell him a book, and he's turning the tables and peddling his surefire writing secrets to me. I toy with the idea of telling him that John Grisham coached me but figure it isn't worth the effort. And in his last comment, he confirms my leftover theory. When I ask him what he thought of my ending, he says, "I didn't get that far. I figured if Gernert didn't like it, why would I?"

So now it's mass submission time. Grisham got his agent with a mailed query, but that was thirty years ago, before the world started writing novels. Back when writers had to painstakingly hunt and peck on Smith Coronas, fiddle with pesky typewriter ribbons, and stain their fingers juggling carbons. When he was a delegate to the Mississippi legislature, John wrote *A Time to Kill* in longhand on a yellow pad in his spare time. Then he typed it out himself and shipped it to his agent in New York.

Back then the sheer man hours involved in the mechanics of writing a novel discouraged many would-be novelists, but with the advent of computers and printers, the floodgates opened and everyone and his uncle who ever imagined having a novel in them is perched over a keyboard cranking them out, then investing in one of the many books that lists agents and bombarding them with queries.

So a twenty-something English major from Vassar who's interning at a literary agency, let's call it Spear McFadden, is going to be deciding my fate. Whether that's true or not isn't important, but it's at least probable since agents receive such a tsunami of queries they can't afford to have high-salaried

employees sorting through thousands of letters. In all fair-
ness, an agent's first responsibility is to the writers already
on board. Like a waiter with too many tables, if they get
stretched thin, everyone suffers. So agents often find themselves passing on some pretty good stuff just because their
plates are full. But from a writer's point of view, the process
seems arbitrary and capricious.

This leads me to imagine, for instance, that Spear
McFadden relegates the task to a freebie intern like Isabel,
who commutes into the city from her parents' home in
Greenwich. She'll open the letter postmarked Keswick,
Virginia, quickly read the plot synopsis about the lost
nuke and the mad scramble to recover it, decide it's not
for Spear McFadden and toss it along with the enclosed
SASE into Muffy's inbox. Muffy is the intern with the task
of sending out rejection letters.

Three weeks after mailing the query to Spear McFadden
I'm standing in the post office reading Isabel's reaction to my
novel idea from Muffy's form letter. Zapped again.

And again. And again. It goes on for four months until
I finally decide I've had enough of the Muffys and Isabels of
the world and cease sending out queries. Which means it's
time to put *Sleeping Dogs* to sleep.

Well, not quite. One spring day I'm walking through
Nordstrom, and I get a call from Gernert. *Has he changed his
mind?* My heart starts racing.

"Hey, David. How're you doing?"

"I'm fine, thanks. Just checking to see what's happened
with your novel."

I tell him the story about the agent who tried to sell me the novel-writing course. We laugh about it.

And then I go on, "But, no, so far no luck with it." I can't decide whether John asked him to call me or he's just interested. John and I spoke only briefly about it. Admittedly, it's a touchy subject. Neither of us wanted to open that wound. He said he knew that David passed on it. Of course I acted positive about all the queries I was sending out, and that was that.

I thank David for his interest and hang up, stopping at the tie section, pulling out a couple, feeling like I'm dangling in the wind. *So this is how it ends*, I think. *Not with a bang but with a whimper in Nordstrom's neckwear department. I pull the plug and poof! The novel goes away. Two years of effort down the drain. All the hopes and dreams dashed.*

Though I've started the outline for another novel, my heart's not in it. "The handwriting's on the wall," as the saying goes. *Maybe you ought to give up this dream of writing a novel and get a real job.*

But first I decide to kick it around with the guys.

"You're grieving," Joe tells me the next Tuesday evening we get together. "It's natural. It's a real loss to you, and I don't blame you for feeling that way."

Knowing how much effort I've put in, and having followed the ups and downs of writing the novel, everyone in the group is helpful.

"You have so many talents, Tony. You're so good at so many things," Bruce says. "I hate to see you run yourself down because this particular novel didn't work."

"Bruce is right," Bob says. "You can do anything you want. Start another novel or go do something completely different."

"I have another one going," I say.

"But you don't seem too excited about it."

"You got that right."

"This is going to be a hard time for you, grieving always is. But you'll get through it and come out fine on the other side."

"It's just hard to know where that is," I say.

"No one likes dealing with uncertainty," Bob says.

"I do have one idea . . ." I say, not entirely sure where I'm heading.

The guys' eyes all brighten.

"The chair of the PEC is on the north side of seventy, and she's been in the job for ten years."

"So you're thinking you'd like to take her place?"

"I don't know. I can't stage a coup. Everyone adores her. She's practically an institution. All the big donors worship at her feet. And it's not like she's doing a bad job."

So I tell the guys I'll be thinking about it and will let them know. They're great. I leave the meeting on an up note.

When I get home, I dry run the idea for Anne.

"If that will make you happy, but I hate for you to give up on your writing."

"Hardly consider it surrendering. I've written six books and spent twelve years doing it."

"And you're convinced there isn't an agent out there you've overlooked?"

"If there is they're in deep cover."

"Are you still planning on using your studio?"

"I'm not sure. I think I want to give that a rest."

"I was afraid of that."

"Why?"

"I guess I got used to having the morning to myself."

"I'll stay out of your hair, and you can always retreat upstairs." We built a loft over the garage as a workplace for Anne's artistic projects. She dabbles in weaving Nantucket baskets, decorating chairs with found bric-a-brac, shredding pop cans and weaving them into fantastic objects like flags, bikinis, and beach balls.

"Still, it's not the same. You went away every morning and I had my own space."

"If I get the PEC job, I'll be on the road a lot. You'll get your space."

"Yeah," she says but doesn't sound convinced. "So how are you going to pull this PEC thing off? Eve is pretty much a fixture up there."

A shrug of the shoulders is the only answer I can come up with. I have absolutely no idea.

CHAPTER 11

Starting Over

Twelve years is a long time to be doing anything. The most I spent at any job was eleven. But I've learned the longer you stay on one track, the harder it becomes to imagine changing your profession. And like anything in life, part of commitment to a single direction means conviction, immersion, honing your skills, and getting damn good at what you do. Yet there's a companion downside—you end up wearing blinders, becoming oblivious to other possibilities.

Advertising was such an intense and all-consuming occupation I had to live and breathe it every minute. I couldn't relax while watching a football game on TV because I'd be analyzing the commercials. I used to drive Anne crazy shopping in the grocery store because I'd lag behind in the aisles checking cereal packaging or lingering in front of Gatorade displays. Since everyone loves to talk about ads, cocktail parties degenerated into endless shoptalk for me. Even after I made the decision to quit, the business stayed in my blood. Only after a couple years in rural Virginia did I begin to wake up to the fact that there was more to life than peddling bottles of shampoo and strategizing for presentations.

I began to notice that yellow finches gradually turned a shade of brown as the weather became colder and that oak trees retained their lower leaves until spring when the new ones force the old to shed. Foxes prowl the fields at dusk, and while both hawks and vultures circle high overhead looking for prey, hawks flap their wings, while vultures leave them open to glide around.

So I give up trying to sell my novel. I abandon my writing and stop going to my studio. Twelve years of living closer to nature frees me up to imagine setting out on a new path. With money out of the equation, the options become clearer. It's not how much you can make doing this or doing that, but what's your passion? What's really going to make you happy? How are you going to make the most out of your remaining time?

I print out Frost's poem about two roads diverging in a wood and tack it to the wall of my studio. *I took the road less traveled by. And that has made all the difference.* It's time for me to take a new direction. Hang up the laptop and devote my time to the PEC. Not like quitting hasn't worked for me before. I left Yale to go into the Peace Corps, ducked out of the film biz into advertising, gave up the ad game to write novels, and fled the city to live in the country. So far reinventing myself has played out nicely.

Even so, it's nerve-rattling. A full month goes by before I summon sufficient resolve to call Chris at the PEC. I keep sorting and resorting the options. *Maybe if I hung in and tried just one more novel—the seventh time's the charm? Or I pick up the name of a new agent in the* New York Times, *and wonder, should I query her?*

I have to face it. I don't have the knack Grisham does. My dialogue is wooden, I tell instead of show, and I struggle with plots. As the song says, you gotta know when to hold 'em, and know when to fold 'em.

I remember back to my McDonalds days in advertising and listening to Ray Kroc talk about getting his hamburger stand going. "I was okay at selling Mixmasters but I was fifty-six and wasn't setting the world on fire. When I saw what the McDonald brothers were doing, I said to myself, I can sell the hell out of this idea."

Figuring I can do a great job at marketing PEC and maybe save a little bit of the world in the process, I finally bite the bullet.

"The next time you come down to Charlottesville," I say to Chris, "drop by the house. There's something I want to talk with you about."

He doesn't miss a trick. "What about tomorrow? You free in the afternoon?" He knows I wouldn't ask him for a meeting unless something was up.

The next day I unveil my plan. "I figure if I can't sell a novel with Grisham looking over my shoulder, it's time to try something else," I tell Chris. "I have deep respect for Eve and all that she's done for us, but as we've discussed, you need another set of hands on the tiller. The board needs new leadership, and we need to get the marketing thing going. And I'm willing to take it on."

Chris's reaction surprises me. "Terrific. I'll call Eve and tell her," he says.

"Not sure I'm ready for that," the ad guy in me responds. "I think we should kick it around some more, talk about how the board will react to the idea, and gameplay the whole idea some more."

"Whatever you want," Chris says, and I can't quite decide what that means. But the next day I find out.

"Hi, Tony. It's Eve," says the familiar voice at the other end of the line. "Chris told me about the idea of you becoming chairman, and that's fine with me."

"Look, Eve," I tell her, "the last thing I want to do is to push you out."

"I don't take it that way at all. Chris thinks it's a good idea, and so do I. I've done it long enough, plus I think you'd make a great chair."

"Thank you, but I think we need to give it some time."

"Sure, whatever you want works for me."

And we leave it there, which is where I want it. The idea's been broached, so it will inevitably leak out, and there will be reactions that I can gauge before moving forward. What I don't know is that in the next two months, my plan will be thrown off course by two sudden tragedies.

Our shade garden is a couple hundred yards from the house, down an incline, and on the other side of the driveway, bordering the all-weather stream our farm is named for, Chopping Bottom. We've tamed the landscape over the years from a jungle of overgrown weeds, brambles, and junk trees to two mulched and manicured gardens, one running twenty yards along the swale perpendicular to the stream, the other meandering along its bank the length of a tennis court. The shady sections are planted with hostas and other low-light plants like arum, hellebore, and Solomon's seal, and the sunnier areas have lilies, roses, hibiscus, and iris. Across the stream, the land is wooded and rises up dramatically so the garden is semi-enclosed and shaded with tall trees.

With the stream gurgling over its rocky bed, it's a peaceful and relaxing spot. We've created a circle of lounge chairs around a fire pit of fieldstones, and we often take a bottle of wine down on a summer evening and enjoy a glass or two to relax with the dogs while we marvel at the garden's serenity and beauty.

On that Fourth of July, Anne's sister, Richie, and my brother, Peter, who live in Boston and happen to be married (making my wife also my sister-in-law), are with us for the weekend. We take drinks and a platter of hors d'oeuvres down to the shade garden with us, anticipating Ellie's arrival to join us for cocktails and dinner. When we see her Subaru approach and slow to make the right turn down the grass incline to the shade garden, we get up to greet her. She's driven the sixty yards down to the garden at least ten times before, but this time as she makes the turn something happens.

Though it's still a blur, we decide later that it couldn't have taken more than four or five seconds. For some reason, instead of braking, Ellie hits the accelerator and comes careering down the hill straight at her two daughters and their husbands. At the last second, her direction changes slightly, and she veers away from us and smashes head on into a maple tree not eight feet from where we're standing. There's a huge crash followed by the tinkling of broken glass and the whoosh of antifreeze escaping from the busted engine. We rush to the driver's side and Ellie, collapsed over the exploded air bag but ever the gracious southern lady, says in a faltering voice, "Sorry to have wrecked such a beautiful evening."

Ellie doesn't make it through the night. A tear in her aorta from the collision is the direct cause, but it is for the better as she has multiple injuries that would make recuperation at her age long and difficult. She would have hated that.

Just a couple of weeks earlier, Ellie had run into a friend of ours at the supermarket and told her how much she enjoyed the music Marcia and her group performed at a recent church service. And Ellie told Marcia she wanted her to play at her funeral. Marcia's reaction was "Don't be silly." Little did she know that ten days later, she would be standing up in front of the congregation singing "Swing Low, Sweet Chariot."

Ellie went out the way she wanted with her life celebrated in a down-home funeral with everyone joyously clapping and singing. We buried her next to her husband in the graveyard behind the church where they were married. It's standing-room only in the church, and when Anne and I walk out after the service, we see the five guys from my men's group, Joe, Bob, Dan, Bruce, and Tom. Although they didn't know Ellie personally, they were there to support me and my wife.

All of us are devastated, stunned, and struggling to make sense of a tragedy that happened instantaneously right in front of our eyes. Our children flock to the farm for the funeral and stay for a couple days, so their presence is some solace.

Trying to return to normalcy, Peter and I pick up the bits and pieces of glass and plastic strewn around the base of the tree so our wives don't have to look at them. There is a light gray discoloration of the bark where her bumper hit that we can't do anything about. None of us spend any time down at the shade garden.

A few weeks later, Anne admits it's too painful to stay on the farm. "I just can't keep driving by that tree six times a day," she says. So we start the process of putting it on the market. Still trying to find a way to cope with Ellie's death, Anne confides that she's having trouble dealing with what would have been her mother's eighty-eighth birthday coming up in December. She suggests we get out of Dodge and head to Paris. We both love the place, I speak good French, and there's a spiffy little apartment in the Marais we like to rent. So it's Christmastime in France for the two of us.

I've put my PEC plans on hold to help Anne through this tough time, but ten days before we leave for Paris, I get a disturbing call from Chris. That morning, Eve Fout had an appointment for a cardiac checkup in Charlottesville. Tough old bird that she is, she drove herself down to the UVa hospital, went through the procedure, was told her doc would give her the results, and was sent home. As she got in her car in the parking lot a resident rushed out and told her they found something they didn't like.

Eve goes on the operating table, and the results aren't good. Her family is with her in the hospital. Chris tells me it's a matter of time. After a few difficult days, Eve passes away. The December PEC board meeting is scheduled while Anne and I are in France. I drive up to Warrenton to talk with Chris.

"Go on your trip," he tells me. "I'll tell the board that you and I and Eve discussed the chairmanship and it's what she would have wanted. There won't be any problem."

CHAPTER 12

No Problem?

It was Thomas Wolfe in *You Can't Go Home Again* who first made the observation, "The end of something is always the beginning of something else."

While Anne and I are on the plane flying back from Paris (a year after David put a bullet in my novel), I am unanimously elected chairman of the Piedmont Environmental Council.

Wouldn't you know it but the shit immediately hits the fan. Not only are we engaged in the toughest and most expensive fight in our existence, which involves trying to defeat the proposed power line that will run across many conserved properties, there are definite signs the economy is hitting the skids. So while we're spending hundreds of thousands on outside energy and transmission experts to help us make our case, there's a real concern that as the economic downturn unfolds, it will become harder and harder for us to raise money to both support the campaign and keep the doors open.

I'm a creative guy, not a financial wizard. Spreadsheets are gobbledygook to me, and profit-and-loss statements make me woozy, even though I ran a 200–person agency with more than 180 million in billings. Plus fundraising isn't my strong suit. While I don't wish I were back in my studio writing novels, I do wonder whether I should have taken the vineyard route.

But I'm in it up to my ears, so I have no choice but to forge ahead. I go north to our Warrenton headquarters a couple of times a week for meetings, strategy, marketing, and my favorite, financials.

In the meantime, we crack the code on the power line.

If the power carried by the new line isn't needed in Virginia, why are they so insistent on building it? Power transmission is an arcane business practiced by a small number of experts and engineers. Most people's understanding stops at the wall switch. But when you hire the right people and really dig down, interesting insights come to light.

There are almost twenty coal-fired power plants in the Ohio Valley, huge, hulking installations built thirty and forty years ago that were grandfathered from the Clean Air Act because it supposedly would have been too expensive to clean up their emissions.

So there is a bunch of coal-fired power produced by plants that were written off balance sheets years ago—cheap juice from coal produced inexpensively. If companies can get their ratepayers to pay for new transmission lines, they can make scads of money selling low-cost electricity to voracious markets in the east. All at zero financial risk to them.

Chris baptizes it "Coal by wire." It's brilliant—absolutely true and right on the money. Now we have a new framing that's a clarion call to energize our supporters and change the course of the debate. A greedy corporation is going to desecrate our landscape with a power line to enable them to sell power to New York and New England that's produced by burning coal in the Ohio Valley. Not only will the Virginia ratepayers have to foot the bill for the new line, we'll also have to put up with the visual degradation and breathe the pollution drifting into Virginia from the Ohio Valley. We get screwed twice and have to pay for it! Talk about a bad deal.

"Coal by wire" becomes our new mantra, and we get more than a thousand people to show up at a rally at Robert Duvall's farm. Chris speaks, the Oscar-winning actor gives a rousing talk, and people write checks and drop them in buckets we've provided. We're over the hurdle that had people sitting on their hands, and we've raised a bunch of money, but it's still an uphill fight.

Months later, we get the State Corporation Commission decision. Despite the holes we poked in their case, they bought Dominion's contention that the line was needed. And the utility doesn't waste any time. Almost the next day landowners hear the roaring of chain saws as crews start widening the right of way.

"I can't believe how big the goddamn things are," Marie Ridder, one of our board members whose property is affected, says when Dominion starts erecting the towers. "They can be seen from everywhere on my beautiful farm. It's a crying shame."

And to add to the pain, the economy tanks, the Dow plunges, property values nosedive, and red ink seeps across our books. You can almost hear our donors' wallets slamming shut. And just when I start thinking things can't get any worse, we get more bad news.

Rumors surface that Walmart is going to build a store right across the road from the Wilderness Battlefield in the southern part of the Piedmont. A Walmart Supercenter cheek by jowl with hallowed ground where almost thirty thousand Union and Confederate soldiers lost their lives seems like the ultimate travesty, as well as setting a terrible precedent for historic sites across the country. We'll have to fight that one too, which means another lawsuit and more money.

I'm desperate, so I ask John Grisham to lunch and level with him, telling him that unless we dig up some quick cash, we're going to have to cut a third of our people and drastically reduce our operating effectiveness. He knows we have a crackerjack staff that make peanuts and work their asses off. Says he'll get back to me. Three days later, he and Renée toss us a life preserver. Thanks to the Grishams, the PEC lives to fight another day.

We thought after eight years of Bush and Cheney, the environment would finally have friends in D.C. But determined to give the country more renewable energy, the Obama Administration comes up with plans for vast wind farms across the Dakotas and determines more transmission capacity is needed to run the power from west to east. When we look at the first maps, it's worse than we imagined. New lines are strung like spaghetti from the far west to New England. And we know exactly what we'll get when we oppose them—what, is the PEC against clean energy?

Fortunately we come up with a rejoinder, another perfect framing device. We discover the proposed lines run over coal deposits and coal-fired power plants. Instead of facilitating clean energy, since power produced from coal is less costly than wind-generated electricity and people are going to buy the cheap juice first, the lines would actually be promoting coal. It's another variation on "coal by wire."

I tell Chris to jump in his Prius and head up to the Hill to make our case. At first, legislators, lobbyists, and energy experts look at him like he's crazy, but the more people he talks to, the more our point of view gains traction.

"What you want to do is string wind farms up and down the East Coast," Chris tells them, "not out in the boonies. The most dependable wind resources are right offshore. You put them far enough out so they're not an eyesore, then you run short undersea connections to the existing grid along the coast, saving billions in transcontinental lines and putting power right where the people are."

At a conference, he buttonholes a friend who's a biggie in Google's energy unit, and for two nights Chris makes the case to him, turning him from a skeptic to a convert.

Jumping ahead almost two years to 2010, Google announces it's putting five billion dollars into an undersea transmission line running from Virginia to New Jersey to facilitate building wind farms off the East Coast. Whether Chris had anything to do with it or not, we don't know. But a good idea finally finds its time.

Dominion's hardly got the first power line up when we see another coming. Two power lines and a Walmart. And this in the middle of a deep recession. Normally we'd be facing threats of new developments and road projects, but since there's no money to build either, the challenges morph into power lines and big-box stores.

The financial situation is a nagging concern. The foundations that provide a good deal of our support are down by thirty and forty percent. Their annual contributions dry up. Individual donors all sing the same song, "Sorry, Tony, this hasn't been a very good year for us." It seems like we're heading into a perfect storm, and I'm wondering whether we're up to it. Will I go down in PEC history as the chair who presided over the organization's demise?

Fortunately, in the summer of '09 we get a windfall. Five years ago, we fundraised to buy an important chunk of land in Northern Virginia. Someone makes an offer that's reasonable for the times, and we accept. So our books go into the black, and we make it through another year.

Whew! I'm thinking. *I'm certainly no Warren Buffett, but so far so good. Two rough years and we're still alive and kicking.*

Odd thing is I'm not missing writing at all. I go up to my studio every six months or so, and that's only to check on things and sweep up the ladybugs that hold regular conventions there. It's eerie, with all my notes for *Sleeping Dogs* pushpinned to the walls, sticky notes detailing David's good news and bad news, my Apple Cube and color monitor forlornly sitting on the minimalist Italian writing stand. Just blasts from the past holding no more emotional attachment to me than the photos of me from *Ad Age* and the shot of my Yale freshman football team.

Then I get an email. It's a request from the editor of *The Piedmont Virginian*, asking if I'll write an autobiographical piece on transitioning from ad man to conservationist. *Why not?* I crank it out, it's short, just over a thousand words, and send it to him. When the magazine comes out, I give it a read. *Nice piece,* I think. *I like the tone. It's an honest, straightforward recounting of the ups and downs in life that have led me to where I am.*

I don't think another thing about it until one person, then two, then five, then ten and twelve stop me to remark how much they enjoyed the article. That gives me an idea.

No, I think, *that's crazy. How boring would that be? A book about writing a book, c'mon.*

But the thought lurks in the back of my mind, and I say to myself, *What the hell? Give it a try.*

It's been almost three years since I euthanized *Sleeping Dogs.* One August day I drive up to the studio and turn the air on full blast, forgetting how long it takes to cool the place down. Sweating like a bandit, I write about five pages. *Not bad.*

The next day I write another three and the next a couple more. *Hmm, coming along. Maybe it could work. Am I actually getting bitten by the damn writing bug again? Is it some invidious disease lying dormant in your system that like the seventeen-year locust suddenly surfaces and starts buzzing around in your brain? Haven't you failed enough at writing?* I ask myself. Then I remember a quote from Mary Pickford, "The thing we call failure is not the falling down but the staying down." *What the hell?* I'm thinking. *What's wrong with giving it another try?*

"What are you doing up in your studio?" Anne asks. "I've seen you head up there a couple times."

"It's a secret."

"Look, I'm happy to see you using it, but I've got to tell you—if you're starting another book, I've got some real problems with that." I'd convinced my wife to launch a flower arranging tutorial business on the web. A subscription service showing people how to do easy but classy arrangements. "Here you've talked me into this Fearless Flowers business. You can't leave me in the lurch."

"I wouldn't do that."

"That would piss me off big time."

"Nothing that's going to get in the way, I promise." I can't tell her because I'm not sure the idea's even going to work. And even if it does, there's a huge hurdle I have to jump before I go any further.

I check with my men's group guys. As always, they're encouraging.

"It's a great idea. If you can keep the tone you had in the *Piedmont* piece, that would be pretty interesting," Dan says. "I really liked that."

"Go for it. If it works, it could be awesome," Joe says.

Yet they have the same caution I have.

Bob spells it out, "You have to check it through with Grisham and make sure he's okay with it. Don't want to get halfway through and have him pull the plug."

I have no idea how John's going to react. He gets more publicity than he wants. Everybody's after him for everything—money, endorsements, speaking engagements—he's had to become a pro at saying no. So he could shut my project down in a second with a quiet, "I'd rather you wouldn't." And that would not be an unexpected reaction from him. But I can't dillydally any longer. If he's going to do a thumbs down, there's no point in spending any more time on it.

"John, it's Tony," I say on the phone. We BS a bit, and then I invite him to lunch.

Our normal hangout went belly up, so now John has a regular table at Hamilton's on the Downtown Mall, which is just a hop, skip, and jump from his office at Oakwood Books.

I start by telling him how much I liked his latest, *The Confession*. "But I tell you, I thought you'd dug yourself one helluva hole there."

"Yeah, it's tough when you kill off your protagonist two-thirds of the way through."

"Still, you pulled it off."

"Thanks, took me a long time to figure out how."

"Hey, I have an idea I want to run by you."

"Fire away."

"So the editor of *The Piedmont Virginian* asked me to write a piece on how an ad guy became a conservationist. I talked about the ad biz, the experience of writing the novel with you, how I got started with the PEC, and all that. And I had a lot of people coming up to me and saying, 'I enjoyed the thing you wrote in *Piedmont Virginian*.' So that gave me an idea—writing a book about writing a book with you. The whole process from start to finish. I started sketching it out, and I think I can make it work. But I obviously need your okay."

"Go for it," John says.

"It's going to be tough to pull off without using your critiques. Like watching grass grow if I don't. Would you let me include them?"

"By all means—no privacy issues whatever."

"Jeez, thanks."

"I'll even edit it for you."

"Wow, great! I'd appreciate that."

"No problem," John says.

We wrap up lunch, split the check, leave, and say goodbye.

I watch John sauntering down the Mall toward his office. Someone stops him, as they often do, and he makes polite conversation for a minute or two. I'm thinking, *John said, "I'll even edit it for you."* Wasn't it almost seven years ago that John and I had a similar lunch with the same outcome?

And then I chuckle as I hear myself thinking, *Here we go again. Some people never learn.*

EPILOGUE

After my trials and tribulations writing *Sleeping Dogs*, I never imagined I'd find myself back in my studio writing five days a week. But when *Writing with the Master* was picked up by Skyhorse, and the publisher also decided to bring out *Sleeping Dogs*, I had renewed energy as a writer as well as a nagging curiosity about my earlier novels. Problem was they were on floppy discs, and none of my computers would recognize them. Were they destined to remain on the unpublished slagheap, or was there gold in those old floppies?

So I asked my computer wizard to see if he could resurrect them. Fortunately, he had a compatible machine, and one day this past spring he delivered two of my stillborn novels to me. I was literally blown away by both. After gathering dust in my studio for over a decade, not only did they hold up, they were some of the best writing I'd ever done.

Ads for God is a hilarious sendup of advertising that might have been before its time when I wrote it in the mid-'90s, but after the success of *Mad Men* and other emerging shows like *The Pitch* and *The Crazy Ones,* it feels fresh and relevant again.

And its companion, *Say Something Funny,* is a takeoff on reality TV, the story of a down-on-his-luck comic on the lam from a nasty bunch of hit men who holes up in an old fogies' home, sort of a Jackie Gleason at Sylvan Glen.

Both have inspired me to go back where I began almost twenty years ago, writing comic novels. I'm now at work on another ad biz story, this one titled, *Client from Hell.* Funny thing is, even after two years of attending John's Guantanamo Bay Writing Camp, I'm not using outlines. Though they may work for him, I found they are a force-fit for me. So I'm composing plot as I go along, mindful of the many lessons I learned from him.

Who would have thought that a nonfiction book about writing a thriller would have brought me full-circle to writing comic novels again? As T. S. Eliot once wrote, "The end of our exploring will be to arrive at where we started, and to know the place for the first time."

So things are good down on the farm. Anne's climbed over her mother's passing, and we're back to enjoying rural life. PEC forced Walmart to find a new site, shut down a second proposed power line, and our bottom line has never looked better. Now it's on to fighting the threat of uranium mining in Virginia and a huge new beltway skirting D.C. to the west. Not to mention a vampire road in Charlottesville we killed off years ago, but even with a stake through its heart it's somehow back to life.

Plus ça change, plus c'est la même chose, but I'm having the time of my life doing it! And all because of one lunch with John Grisham and a book about lost bombs.